BEYOND SURPRISE

Kenneth Magee

Inspiring Voices books may be ordered through booksellers or by contacting:

Inspiring Voices
1663 Liberty Drive
Bloomington, IN 47403
www.inspiringvoices.com
1-(866) 697-5313

ISBN: 978-1-4624-0264-9 (sc)
ISBN: 978-1-4624-0263-2 (e)

Library of Congress Control Number: 2012913772

Printed in the United States of America

Inspiring Voices rev. date: 07/31/2012

DEDICATION

I dedicate this book totally to my wife, **Jo Anne Tuning Magee.** You have stood by me through years of hard work, long absences, my battling compassion fatigue by following redbone hound dogs, and my being gone for months to troubled parts of the world. You are spectacular and through your giving to me have also given to thousands.

I love you much.

CONTENTS

ACKNOWLEDGMENTS

Many thanks to:

Fellow writers at Klamath Writers' Guild. You have patiently listened to countless readings and offered excellent suggestions.

Cheryl Tamplen for long hours of careful editing. You have shown me both general thoughts and minutia that needed changing—things that I would never have seen. May your astounding expertise continue to benefit other authors in the years to come.

William Huntsman, for your encouragement and knowledge. Your suggestions and insights in arranging the stories and putting finishing touches on the book have helped immensely. A book should be written about how you secretly lift thousands of lives by your own writing.

Lynn Vanderzalm of Medical Teams International, who helped me with accuracy, information, and excellent editing expertise. I much appreciate you.

Medical Teams International for superb support in all the facets of travels to disaster areas.

And to fellow travelers into a hurting world. Many of you could easily have a book written about your adventures and kindnesses. Here are some of the names from my times on other parts of our globe: Ron, Mike, and Donna; Marti, Kristin, Dennis, Jackie, and Nancy; Tom, Carol, Rick, Carrie, Deanna, Sandi, Neil, Bill, Tom, and Donna; Ken Jr., Otto, Valerie, and Matt; Mary, Kirk, Leo, Steve, Tami, Aaron, Betty, and Terry; Mary, Lorie, and Moses;

Wendy, Oren, Jenna, Norma; Lou, Susan, and Mike. Thank you, and others, immensely. Some have traveled with me several times. And I send much gratitude to those from other parts of the world—too many to name.

INTRODUCTION—
STORIES TEACH EVERYONE

A large part of my role as a physician has been to listen–both here in Klamath Falls, Oregon, and in my journeys with disaster teams to hurting parts of the world. Approaching danger and suffering people with the realism of "we are here to help where we can, but we also want to learn from you," opens doors. Richness flows from experiences working with co-laborers of various faith and medical backgrounds, mostly with Medical Teams International (formerly Northwest Medical Teams). Challenges mixed with learning, and even a bit of humor, become great adventures.

As I finished this book I marveled at some of the teachers who helped me along the way:

- Nergis in Iraq, pursued by Saddam Hussein—with intent to kill her.
- John Mohammed Nayab, at large personal risk, my protector in northern Afghanistan.
- Responding to letters from George W. Bush on Afghanistan and Iraq.
- A dirty, bedraggled Afghan burro made into a hero.
- Flomo, a tiny Liberian boy near death, carried by his mother.
- My "almost a people," redbone hound, Ginger, gone for thirty years, who still teaches me.

- Finding it very tough to get the boot off cowboy Joe's sore foot.
- The story behind "the burnt log" rediscovered forty years later on remote Swan Lake Rim.
- The rescue of two lost nurses in the unique Gearhart Wilderness area.

All these and many more are beyond surprise.

I am thankful for the privilege of learning the ways of other cultures: the Liberian handshake, when and where to take off your shoes in Uzbekistan, the proper hand in Sumatra with which to wave and eat, appropriate sitting distance from a Turkish patient of the opposite sex, and how to catch and consume Ugandan flying ants—interpreted by Lou.

It is easier to see the shaping of an inner journey as I look back on my past. Many years before, as a bashful farm boy, I had accepted the objective in life of giving God the best I could. In fact, I took a piece of balsa wood, covered it with golden paint and printed with a black marker THE BEST YOU'VE GOT on one side. For years it hung on my bedroom wall as a reminder.

As time passed, in spite of my many imperfections, I became very aware of God's smile, began to consider further education in medicine, and pursued a young lady who became my wife.

Initial attempts to go on to medical school were interrupted by the Korean War, and working as a scrub nurse at a station hospital in the army, then three years of teaching elementary school. I continued to feel God's nudges toward medicine.

This ultimately led to eight more years of intensive study in medical school, internship, and residency. I then worked as an internal medicine physician in Klamath Falls, Oregon, for many more years, backing away from that heavy load at age sixty-five. I continued part-time work as an assistant professor in a family practice residency program under Oregon Health and Sciences University, and have worked as a Klamath Hospice medical director for about ten years. Through all of these years my objective made as a quiet teenager remained.

Near the beginning of my career, I had felt a definite draw toward countries of the developing world. This brought fulfillment beginning four years after leaving full-time active practice when I began journeying with Medical Teams International's disaster response teams to many parts of the world.

My family played a huge role in these expeditions–parents, siblings, wife, children, and grandchildren. I especially honor my wife, who put up with these absences for long weeks and months, and the reality of sometimes not knowing with certainty if I'd return.

On coming back from northern Afghanistan the first time, I carried a large envelope with a letter and several small gift items to a family whose physician husband and dad still worked in that war zone. I met them in the waiting area at Portland International Airport. It stirred me deeply as they opened the envelope, caressed the gifts, and read. His laughing wife and his two young daughters virtually danced in tremendous jubilation. I pay immense tribute to other medical personnel with whom I worked who were missed by their families and friends.

I've been enriched by the stories of patients and friends from years ago to the present. May these stories inspire you to give your best to God and to also open and share your memories with family and others.

LEARNING—TAUGHT BY A DOG

"Ken, I haven't felt any movement for three or four days." My wife, Jo Anne, rested one hand on her abdomen that January morning. A multitude of thoughts tumbled through my head there in our small apartment near Bernalillo County Indian (BCI) Hospital in Albuquerque, New Mexico. Though the apartment was old and dingy and smelled strongly of the tobacco smoke of prior residents, we were glad to have such an economical place close to my work in which to live. "After the kids are up, you'd best take the car over to see Dr. Brian and get checked. Maybe our neighbor, Lucy, can watch Jeanne and Noel for a bit." We quickly agreed.

At 6:00 a.m., I was hurrying to get to waiting responsibilities as an intern on my obstetrics rotation. Days were long, and my nights were sometimes totally interrupted. Already in that month, I'd delivered over ninety babies. No doubt, more would be waiting. Fortunately, a resident physician, Dr. Martinez from Colorado, was doing an added learning year in OB at County Indian Hospital and was there to help. As I left for the short jog to the hospital, my mind and emotions fluctuated back and forth. But then, on entering the hospital door, my attention fastened on the work of the day.

It was a busy day—delivering a breech baby with little buttocks appearing first and needing considerable straightening to help her arrival; helping with a C-section, necessitated by very slow progress and the baby's heartbeat slowing to a critical level; and twins, a boy and a girl, both arriving with healthy squalling. After my tying and cutting umbilical cords, the nurse wiped the twins off, and I had the pleasure of placing them in the arms of a relieved and smiling mother while the nurse went to get the woman's husband.

That day, I again noted how strongly family backgrounds affected individuals in labor. One young lady, who was very early in her process, screamed with each light contraction. When asked about the pain, she revealed, "I'm supposed to cry and scream." Later, I left the room of a Navajo lady who was midway through her labor. Returning a bit later, she was squatting in the corner of the room, bearing down. She never whimpered a bit. Through an interpreter, she told me that this was the way they did it at home. We persuaded her to climb back into bed, and a nurse checked her progress frequently.

After sundown, tired but hurrying home, I found Jo Anne and my two young children. Dr. Brian had told her that our baby was dead, having no heartbeat or movement, and would probably deliver in a few days. It was a boy. Jo had called her mom back in Oregon, and she was on her way.

After our children were in bed, we sat close together on the small, scruffy old couch, held each other, and talked. We had previously selected a boy's name, John Evert, in honor of our two fathers, both of huge influence in our lives. In my thinking, John Evert was now gone. Jo wept.

Jo's mom arrived soon, and four days from seeing Dr. Brian, there was a firm nighttime nudge and then my wife's voice: "The baby is coming." We dressed and softly wakened her mother. She'd watch the children.

Upon checking into the maternity unit at BCI, we were pleased to be told that Dr. Martinez was the one on call. Contractions were coming regularly about every minute, so he took her directly to the delivery room. My wife was given some help with pain medicine and was put up in stirrups with the familiar light blue drapes.

We waited while Jo labored, and the head of the little one rapidly appeared. His body was blue, and there was not the least sign of life. Dr. Martinez severed the umbilical cord, wrapped the tiny body of little John in a soft blue towel, and placed him on the nearby instrument table. Jo slept. I felt sad, but there were no tears.

I stuffed my feelings. When asked, I instructed the nurse to take him away. He was cremated, and his ashes were scattered. I never inquired as to where the scattering took place. Jo's mother helped much, and a few friends visited. Jo wept and wept.

Five years later, we had moved to Klamath Falls in southern Oregon. It was a good situation for both my family and me. Mountains with snowy peaks, pine forests, deer, and huge flocks of snow geese were only a few of the many beauties of the area. The kids walked about a mile to Peterson Grade School. We rapidly became involved in our church. I was one of two internists in that large area and loved caring for people. Dr. Howard and I knew we practiced good medicine.

Then Jo was again pregnant, and we began looking ahead. Ultrasound showed it was a boy, and we named him Jedidiah Harmon—once again, family names. At six and a half months, Jedidiah was found to be having trouble. Activity was decreased, and the heartbeat was far too slow. Our obstetrician, Dr. Bell, decided to do a C-section, realizing that the chance of the little one surviving was exceedingly small. We gave our okay.

A short time later, Jedidiah was delivered and immediately was placed in an incubator. I stayed with Jo after the surgery, and Dr. Bell came by to talk. He and a pediatrician felt that if there was the slightest chance of the wee one living, he needed care in a pediatric intensive care unit. A new unit was available in Medford, about seventy miles to the west. We agreed. The little boy was brought by in an incubator for Jo to see before they transferred him. Jo wept. I looked at the statistics and impossibilities.

I pulled away from my busy practice and visited the Pediatric Care Unit in Medford several times. A nurse offered to let me hold the little one, but I declined. I knew that he was failing and that survival chances were essentially nonexistent. My teeth gritted, but my eyes stayed dry, and my arms did not reach out. Again, I stuffed my feelings.

After ten days, a call came. Jedidiah had died. He was cremated, and they scattered his ashes. Again, I did not inquire as to where the ashes might be scattered.

###

We nicknamed her the Terror of the Southern Cascades. I had returned to running redbone hounds soon after coming to Klamath Falls in 1967; she was one of them. Ginger was her real name, and her fur was some of the softest and silkiest I had ever felt. It was winter when we got her, and she lived inside with us until the weather warmed. She seemed to understand English and was easily trained. For about two years, Ginger seemed to think she was "a people." She would generally stay with us while listening to the baying dogs trailing a bobcat or bear in the distance. Later, she became the best trail dog that my hunting partner, Steve, and I had. She was actually a gentle dog, and she was especially good at deciphering the hidden scent of bobcats and cougars. Her voice was beautiful, a medium-pitched musical bay, long and drawn out. I can still hear her in my mind, sending me off to work and welcoming me home.

It pleased me when Steve wanted to take her with him and his own redbones to chase cougars in northern Nevada. I was too busy to go. I had to attend some medical meetings. On my return, I found Steve had come home a couple of days earlier and had taken her to a veterinarian. Ginger had followed a cougar track a ways up a steep hillside, and then she slowed and could go no further. She was quite ill. The vet informed me that she had widespread cancer, including cancer in both lungs, and lingered near death. I was devastated and said, "Go ahead and put her to sleep."

I drove my old Toyota north from Klamath Falls and up the gravel road above Hagelstein Park. There, on that ridge, I wept and wept. I thought, "Why didn't I go in where Ginger lay and hold her while she was put to sleep? Then she'd have known I was there and loved her."

As I grieved, it seemed as though an inner voice said to me, "Do you remember those little boys? You could have held them too, but, instead, you stuffed your feelings and acted like a doctor and not a dad."

These terrible realities impacted me deeply—my soul was shaken. It was a deep and meaningful lesson, a turnaround. God's forgiveness helped, but the memories continue to bear much pain.

My expectation is for Jo and me, with family gathered close around, to someday sit with arms around John Evert and Jedidiah Harmon, the four of us together holding Ginger across our laps. As we stroke her, she will lick our hands and snuggle—such soft, silky fur and such a beautiful voice. *Peace* and *joy!*

TURKEY—
AFTERMATH OF CRUSHING EARTHQUAKES

The Anatolian fault has a history of rupturing with very destructive force about every two hundred to six hundred years. It snakes across northern Turkey, just south of the Black Sea. On August 17, 1999, a 7.6 quake hit and was followed by many aftershocks. Thousands died, with estimates ranging from seventeen thousand to fifty thousand. Many others were left homeless.

The Turkish government brought in thousands of shipping containers to make into temporary homes. Northwest Medical Teams International, now called Medical Teams International, combined with World Relief USA and numerous Turkish churches in bringing help. NWMTI's role was to provide ongoing medical assistance. The primary facility was at Derince, with satellite clinics at two other villages near Ismit.

When I arrived in Turkey, months had passed since our first team came in August. I was jarred by the huge number of flattened multistory cement buildings. They covered much of the countryside in northwestern Turkey, near Ismit. Getting out of our car to look closer at an area of rubble, the stench of decaying bodies was still strong. Among tufts of grass, I found a small rag doll.

A NEW ADVENTURE: "COMING HOME" LETTER TO FAMILY AND FRIENDS

As some of you know, I returned from Turkey's splendor and rubble Saturday afternoon. Yesterday was spent mostly sleeping, and in my dreams last night, I was trying to figure out the conversion rates between Turkish lira and American dollars. I felt relieved to waken and realize that I didn't have to do that now. As you know, Paramedic Ron and Dr. Mike traveled with me. I couldn't have asked for better companions. Both have much experience in foreign travel and proved most helpful.

Amid the splendor and antiquity of the Blue Mosque and other ancient buildings in Istanbul (formerly called Constantinople) I felt a bit ill at ease initially. Traffic in and around this city seemed hectic. The streets overflowed with people, cars, and some carts with horses. Traffic moved rapidly, filled with honking, bluffing, and near misses. Stop signs seemed to mean that the other person *might* have the right-of-way. I was learning. Gradually, with shortening of pauses, my Turkish "hello" and "thank you" came easier.

The area east of Istanbul near Ismit had lost about seventeen thousand buildings and nearly fifty thousand people died in the quakes. We saw numerous huts built of residuals from collapsed buildings and sheets of plastic. Our refugee camp near the small town of Derince was composed of containers, like semis carry on their trailers. A wooden door and usually two windows had been placed in each. A tiny wooden porch had been attached to most, and some inhabitants were adding another small side room. The entire camp had one central bathroom, with separate men's and women's ends. They included "squat" toilets, sinks, and cold showers if the water was running. There was a distant warm shower available at times. Ron recalled that he'd gone several days without visiting that shower, and when he came out of the tiny building hearing a group singing "Glory, Glory ..." he thought they must be singing for him.

Our "magnificent" medical clinic consisted of three containers put together in a "T" shape. The bottom became the waiting and classroom area, and the side branches were examining rooms. A single tiny toilet room with an actual sit-down commode hid between the two side arms. Drawings by children exposed their horrible earthquake memories and covered the waiting room walls. On some days the two nurses would teach health and first aid classes. They used puppets and much drama. Most of the people of that part of Turkey were illiterate. They would strain to watch the demonstrations closely, and would sometimes speak and clap with excitement.

Nearby, Hrant, a superb Iraqi interpreter, and I slept in a tiny container on two narrow cots. It lent itself to long talks and much listening. My tiny recorder helped my memory. (Hrant's story follows soon.)

Our days started with a very delicious breakfast—usually a boiled egg, olives, goat cheese, an orange or apple, and Turkish bread. One of our group then led a devotional time. We worked in the clinic through the day interrupted by short but very culturally needful tea breaks (not a bad idea), and a bit of noon lunch. Each morning there would always be a large group of people waiting at the clinic door. One of our interpreters would try to ascertain an order of arrival and being seen. Two days a week we would see only people from Derince, and the other weekdays see anyone. On Tuesdays and Thursdays Dr. Mike and I would alternate going to see displaced people at our two distant small clinics near Ismit. Fridays, the Muslim holy day, and Saturdays were reserved for emergencies only.

It was long enough after the hard quakes that acutely caused physical problems were mostly over. Many people had anxiety and depression, with numerous persons having lost family members, all having lost homes, and most with livelihoods gone. Physical ailments were much like we'd see in the United States: colds, pneumonias, headaches, heart trouble, diarrhea, diverticulitis, appendicitis, tonsillitis, and the like. I did see a lot of people with goiters, as they commonly use noniodized salt. A huge percentage suffered from stomach and acid reflux problems. There were a very few similar to one middle-aged lady from another area who appeared trim but aspired to becoming much heavier. The Turkish government claimed health-care opportunity for all, and I met some excellent physicians. I was favorably impressed by a medical school near Istanbul. However, the refugees were the poorest of the poor and health care was not always easy to access. One lady with cancer told me she would have to wait two years before chemotherapy could be started.

In questioning and examining the Turkish Islamic people I did not know what to expect. Soon after starting, my nurse informed me, "You are sitting too close to the female patients!" So I moved my chair nearer the far wall of the container, and that sufficed. She would, of course, help me in making available whatever was needed for the exam. Generally, the men would pull up the tails of their six shirts and sweaters, exposing a small area of skin. I was amazed how even very elderly patients could climb up on the exam table and sit cross-legged. Their usual ability to do this, or rare lack of it, told me much about their health. As the days went by my level of ease certainly increased, and by the time I left I enjoyed many Turkish hugs and kisses. I miss those.

Farm animals weren't only in the hills around Derince but were also scattered about in the town wherever green grass appeared. Turkish dogs mostly looked mangy and sick. I think I only heard one get up the energy to bark a few times. Gardens with garlic, onions, lettuce, etc., were also frequent wherever there was space.

The hills appeared green and beautiful except for the plethora of dumped garbage along the roadways. This was interesting in that the people mostly seemed very clean. Few birds enlivened the area. I looked forward to a trip into those hills. However, when we did try it, our driver had been a race car driver and drove accordingly. It was a relief to return to Derince.

One of the best things in the camp was the opportunity to be with people from many parts of the world who had come to work with World Relief. The leader of the camps was a South African, an engineer, who'd come by way of England. Others with whom I worked were from Malaysia, Germany, England, Scandinavia, and Turkey itself. The cooks had come from Iran, having fled their country under penalty of death. My two main interpreters were of Romanian-Turkish and Armenian-Lebanese-Turkish backgrounds. I heard so many interesting stories and recorded some.

I think that possibly the greatest accomplishments of our group were the open doors for Ron and Mike to teach basic life support classes. These classes included about 250 of the local police, Mercy International workers in Istanbul, and Ron alone teaching the ambulance people in Istanbul. Hrant, their interpreter, told me, "When we entered a room and one hundred police snapped to attention, I felt like the prime minister."

(In subsequent years Ron and others continued teaching basic life support classes and made associated booklets accessible in many languages. Through these efforts many millions of new people now have this available.)

HEROS: HRANT'S STORY

"Life in Lebanon was good. My father worked as a furrier and a fur expert in the Lebanese way, as my family had for six generations. I was learning the trade. I had a good school to attend and good friends with whom to play football. I remember so well the green mountains with their beautiful and famous cedars, and our summer home. There was large demand for the work of furriers. We made coats for royalty, including the king of Egypt, the king of Jordan, and several princes from Saudi Arabia. Our family was well-known and respected. Then suddenly without warning, when I was eleven, war came to Lebanon.

"I guess I shouldn't have been surprised. This has been my Armenian people's history. We are a people who have lived in areas between the Black and Caspian Seas north of Lebanon, throughout eastern Turkey and western Iran and Iraq, and on down into Syria and Lebanon. Now we are scattered throughout the world. There are perhaps ten million of us left. We have been Christians since about three hundred AD when St. George the Illuminator helped us to change from Zoroastrianism. We have been overrun by many, including the Romans, the Persians, the Turks, and the Arabs. All of my family have lived wars.

"In 1915, the majority of the people living in the southeast region of Turkey called Cilicia, ancient Armenia, were driven into the Arabian Desert (Syria). Hundreds of thousands died there of exhaustion, starvation, and sunstroke. My great-grandfather had a heart attack in this 'chasing' and died. We were thrown out from our homeland, where we had lived for over a thousand years. My ninety-three-year-old grandmother remembers the genocide clearly. It was then that my family settled in Lebanon.

"My grandfather was a master chemist and superb furrier and passed on his knowledge to my father. We prospered and became quite wealthy. Our home in Beirut was beautiful. Our home in the mountains was one of peace. Most Armenians were jewelers, carpenters, or furriers. My family was brought up under the Bible. We prayed and worked. I was educated in the Armenian Evangelical High School in Beirut. As a child I dreamed of becoming a journalist, a foreign minister, or a psychiatrist. I always wanted to help people.

"Like an unexpected storm, war descended on us again on April 13, 1975. At least to my eleven-year-old mind it was without warning. The blasts of explosives, bombs, and land mines, the whistles of shells and small-arms fire, and militia hurrying by our home became familiar. Friends and neighbors disappeared. Some we knew had left for what might be a safer place. Some were gone after their homes were destroyed. We didn't know what had become of many others. The fragrance of flowers and bushes was replaced by the smells of spent powder, the smoke of fires, and decaying flesh.

"I was frightened. My family tried to comfort me and tried to keep a semblance of normalcy. But the sandbags stacked in the windows, to prevent bullets or shrapnel or to prevent someone from throwing in a grenade, were constant reminders of fear. In fact, as the war came closer and then backed away, my father sent us from Lebanon twenty-four different times. These included trips to Germany, Cyprus, Greece, Romania, Canada, England, Switzerland, France, and Turkey. As you can imagine, our family's fortune was rapidly spent. Twice we were robbed in other countries. Once my father's company was robbed, and the insurance company would not pay us for that robbery.

"As I grew older, the danger for me increased. One day I went from the house to seek food for the family. I forgot to take my papers with me. The militia picked me up and hustled me to an area where they had about thirty-five Arab men. I protested that I was a Christian. But they would not believe me. We were treated very badly. Our hands were tied behind our backs, and we were forced to kneel down. One by one the other prisoners were shot in the head. I was frantic! Finally the captain of the unit began asking me questions and was convinced that I was a Christian. They let me go with the advice that I must never leave home again without my ID papers. That day and its terror have never left my mind.

"A short time later, at the age of seventeen, I was kidnapped by the militia and put in the army. I had already witnessed too much killing and was convinced that I wouldn't participate in more. I escaped and contacted my father. Together we took the remainder of our family fortune in a briefcase and determined to leave Lebanon for good. We had been treated well by the Israeli merchants in the past and resolved to head for Israel's border.

"We knew that before we reached Israel we would have to pass through several Lebanese checkpoints. If they discovered I was a deserter, they would shoot me, but if I stayed in Lebanon they would shoot me. I and my father prayed and determined to try. We walked right through three Lebanese checkpoints and were not stopped or questioned. It was as if they did not see us. Finally we got to the Israeli outpost. There the captain questioned us for about six hours. We explained that to return to Lebanon was death. Those Israeli soldiers in Lebanon were good to us. They finally let us enter their country. From Haifa we journeyed to Istanbul, Turkey, and there gathered our family again.

"We have been glad for a home in Turkey. We have a church family here. In 1992 I met the president of Turkey, Mr. Ozal. He asked me to "Come visit me at any time. I would like to talk with you more." But my father told me, "Don't do that. We are not politicians. We are businessmen."

"I have not had steady work. I have worked at many jobs, but part of some jobs has been to take advantage of others whenever I could, and I have not wanted to do that. I want to treat people well.

"I was married a little over a year ago. When I met my future wife, she was using her uncle's phone number. So I asked for his number, and the first few times I called I would tell her, 'I'm calling to check on your uncle.' We soon got past that stage, and I was able to see her privately. When we got married, we didn't have enough money to pay the rent that was due in a week. As a newly married couple we said, 'God will provide,' and indeed He did, and has continued to do so. I am so grateful for a beautiful and kind and gracious and believer wife.

"I am grateful for the volunteers who served in the earthquake region of Turkey. Most of them were so very kind and happy in receiving my services. The earthquake region of Turkey has taught me important lessons and brought me closer to Him."

(It has been my privilege to follow Hrant through the years since my visits to Turkey. He is fulfilling his dreams of reaching out to suffering peoples of many backgrounds. He is a true humanitarian who lives his beliefs. Ken Magee)

EL SALVADORAN TRAGEDIES

El Salvador is a small Central American country bordered by the Pacific Ocean, Guatemala, and Honduras. It has been plagued by violence for many years. Conflict between rich and poor has existed for a hundred years. Civil war began in 1980 with the government targeting anyone suspected of supporting reform. Death squad killings included unionists, clergy, independent farmers, and university officials. The civil war accounted for nearly one hundred thousand people dying in the latter part of the twentieth century. In many other locales barred windows and high adobe walls topped by razor wire attested to enormous past sources of fear.

It is a land of volcanic mountains—some still active. On January 13, 2001, a strong earthquake hit El Salvador, causing much devastation. Frequent aftershocks followed, and another strong earthquake hit on February 13, centered at a different Salvadoran site.

I traveled with Medical Teams International to El Salvador soon after the devastating earthquake on January 13, 2001. Hundreds died, and many aftershocks followed, adding to the fear already present. Over large areas we found huge piles of rubble caused by those recent quakes. In spite of that, as I experienced El Salvador, I began to see beyond that country's sorrows and have been deeply touched by her resilience and joy.

GLIMPSES OF EL SALVADOR: BEYOND THE TRAGEDY

Our team, working with an excellent and experienced leader, Marti, felt the hope and obvious great appreciation of the people of El Salvador.

As we started our sojourn, we went to a small distressed village and stopped at a tiny clinic to see what might be needed. Unexpectedly, we found a group of about seven men and women sitting around a table in a little patio between fractured walls. They had neat uniforms of grayish-tan, and a young Salvadoran doctor was with them. These were the health promoters for that region. Upon learning of our wish to help in areas without medical help, we found they were not only eager to give suggestions but would guide us through remote roads and trails and make needy people aware of the opportunity. These health promoters added enormous value to our work.

The mayor of a small town gave us a place to sleep. A nearby lady with a tiny store fixed our meals. I especially loved her frozen bananas dipped in chocolate.

Immediately after our arrival, a ten-year-old boy with his fractured leg wrapped in cardboard and string was carried to us by his father. The son's smile appeared and broadened after accompanying us through the complicated process of getting his leg x-rayed and a proper cast applied. Now he could anticipate someday playing soccer again. His dad rode with us to the tent hospital a distance away but forgot his machete in our van. His profound pleasure for our helping his son and our return of the machete furnished us rich payment.

Near the small village of Santa Elena the ground often shook as a nearby volcano spewed smoke and ran red-hot molten lava down its side. While walking to our little clinic, three of us decided to detour through rubble-strewn side streets. All buildings were damaged. Many were only a standing doorway or post. Two ladies stood in front of a mostly intact small shop holding a dipper and large kettle full of cold pink juice. They hoped to sell some to the few passersby on this very warm day. We talked a bit, and they insisted that we each take a plastic bag of cool fruit drink with its tiny straw. Our attempt to pay was met with firm refusals. The drinks were delicious!

A bit farther down that street we met two elderly ladies and a child. Their faces revealed obvious sadness but changed to pleasure upon receiving the small straws and the plastic bags holding the last half of our cool juice.

Roads were often very primitive. We ran aground on a pile of rocks as we left one of our several side-yard clinics. This was a constant possibility, but our skilled driver had remarkably kept us out of trouble to that point. We got out of our van and "all the king's men" (and women), along with some passing conscripts, couldn't get us unstuck. Happily, a driver with his ox team happened by and with an attached line quickly freed our van.

Once we became lost. We'd journeyed through a cooler mountainous region and had come to a large river. We hadn't, however, found the unmarked road leading to our destination. Even our Salvadoran health promoter was unsure. We stopped to ask a fisherman where the village might be. He said, "I'll show you," and gave up his day's fishing to not only show us the primitive road but to also help us with the logistics of that entire day. He wouldn't accept payment.

Nancy, a very kind and experienced American counselor, traveled with us and started many grief support groups. These seemed to stimulate a lot of compassionate interactive support, even in a short time.

After I visited a very ill child in her home, the matriarch was insistent that I be given a live chicken. She used a bit of cord to bind its legs and handed it to me, and I accepted. She would not allow refusal.

El Salvador—so much pain but also much kindness and even hope.

AFTERSHOCKS!

During our stay in El Salvador things shook frequently. Often we'd be wakened at night. By February 2, 2001, more than twenty-five hundred aftershocks had caused additional damage and kept the populace filled with fear. On February 13 we had checked into the airport in San Salvador expecting to fly home soon. As Marti, Kristen, and I waited in the departure area the terminal began to shake. It became severe. Light fixtures fell about us, and a corner of the building fell away. One nearby lady had scalp lacerations. We were told to vacate. As we proceeded rapidly down the off-loading ramp the shaking continued. It was difficult to stand. Just ahead the ramp buckled upward, slapping Marti's foot. It then closed back down but left her in severe pain. Kristen and I tried to assist her. Thankfully our plane was loaded with luggage, and we were permitted to board. We waited while the runway was inspected. Our plane and one other were allowed to take off.

As we flew northward toward home our already enormous tension abruptly increased when the plane suddenly plunged earthward, caught in a huge downdraft. One nearby passenger grabbed my arm and held on tightly during that plunge.

We were able to help Marti by finding a motorized conveyance while changing planes in California. At home, Marti had her foot x-rayed. It was fractured.

EYES OF EL SALVADOR

These Spoke to Me Over and Over

Elena: somber, staring, scarcely blinking; black lashes circling widely rounded, chestnut-shaded eyes. No smile lines on this six-year-old. No response to my attempts to initiate warmth—only a drawing away from this stranger's smile and touch, and a great reluctance to submit to my stethoscope.

What inner grief do those eyes conceal? With parents working in the fields, she had staggered from her home pulling a tiny brother and sister and then watched it shake to rubble behind them. A crushed brother and pet who were buried in adobe bricks were later pulled from it, only to be buried again. Now her bed is of cornstalks surrounded by dark night. Many eyes in El Salvador reflect such memories.

Skinny little dogs, edging closer as we ate our lunchtime sandwiches, watching intently for extra morsels, hoping, begging. One is black and white spotted with only thinly covered bones—seemingly now with no one to claim him, no one to own him. No master. Eyes wishing, pleading, edging closer.

Slouching, hands in pockets, eyes averted, Carlos mumbled almost inaudibly in response to my greeting. He was to be our interpreter. Gradually a bit of his revealed past showed he'd been deported to El Salvador after spending jail time in Los Angeles. He avoided further details. But slowly he warmed. His gaze finally met mine, and he even began to smile. His slouch lessened as his eyes became responsive, not only to me but especially to the passing senoritas, and bit by bit I had glimpses of inner richness.

Julio, walking carefully and reaching with uncertainty for its dim back, eased into his chair. The translator related, "He believes his eyesight is bad." No light was needed to see the residue of years of volcanic dust. Epithelial blinds were creeping across his corneas, and deeper still I saw the white opacities of dense cataracts. Both of these so very curable, and yet with the poverty of this land, so very distant.

Peeking from behind the corner of the caretaker's hut I see a pair of shy, dark eyes. There, high in the hills on a coffee plantation with its canopy of mangos, avocados, and coconut palms, she lives with her parents. I see a bit of her small dirty dress and, at times, a bare foot but mostly wide brown eyes—excited, wondering, and afraid of those visiting gringos.

Eyes, so very much revealed and so very much hidden. I wished a healing touch for each sorrow.

Dennis, an emergency medical technician, is a master at hugging sad-eyed children, of lifting them high, of tickling tummies, of kissing brown cheeks and making those smile lines emerge. This was his eighteenth trip to a devastated part of the world. He was our excellent "pharmacist and driver," but it became obvious what his greatest gift is. After a previous trip to the stricken country of Rwanda-Zaire, upon emerging from his plane in Portland, Oregon, he had been asked for an interview. He could not speak. His inner eyes bore the burden of countless ill, starving, and dying children. Outwardly he could only weep …

May it be that the greatest of healers are those bearing wounds—like Christ, the ones with eyes weeping but filled with love?

THE WAR IN AFGHANISTAN

The Afghan war began October 7, 2001, as armed forces of the United States of America, the United Kingdom, Australia, and the Afghan Northern Alliance launched "Operation Enduring Freedom." The September 11 attack on the United States was a primary driver. The stated goal was that of dismantling the Al-Qaeda terrorist organization, removing the Taliban regime from power, and creating a living democracy. A prelude to the war was the assassination of the primary leader of the Northern Alliance, General Ahmad Shah Massoud, by suicide bombers.

It was into this very unsettled situation that Medical Teams International was called to extend medical help to a huge and suffering internally displaced people (refugee) population. Generals of the Northern Alliance and United Nations personnel helped to open those early doors for our disaster response teams.

JOURNEYS TO AFGHANISTAN—A LENGTHY ROAD

I'd never have believed it three years earlier. Opening before me was the multilocked door of going with Medical Teams International to Afghanistan, a devastated country almost directly on the other side of the world. The events of September 11, 2001, awakened many of us to that needy area, which had suffered through twenty-three years of nearly continuous war.

The Afghanistan opportunity in January of 2002 gave me both a sense of impending adventure and fear. Certainly things would be very different: culturally, we would essentially be in a war zone, and the winter weather was said to be *cold*. There was reality in the fear. The first team from Medical Teams International reported a nearby explosion injuring and killing many people.

All these thoughts resulted in my wrestling with this question: "Am I just a silly old man?" Finally I posed the thought in a letter to my family as follows:

> "Dear Ones, I will be flying out of Portland next Saturday bound for Afghanistan. It has been a difficult decision from the standpoint of its being much more comfortable to stay home, and I sure do especially miss my wife when gone. On the other side of the ledger are some very compelling needs. I fret about my family's wondering, "What is that silly old man up to now?" In the middle of my trying to

hear God, I received several reassurances, such as my friend, Bill Tamplen, telling the story of the boy with five loaves and two fishes who gave all that he had to Christ, and many were fed. I do feel much like that boy. So Dear Ones, do pray for this silly old man.

Much love, Dad, alias Grandpa"

My family responded with a variety of things to ponder. I especially want to share with you this letter from my son, Noel:

> Dear Pa, When men are young they generally think nothing bad can happen to them. When they are older (and wiser) perhaps they understand that what happens to them is not the most important thing. Considered from the outside both sets of circumstances give rise to actions that might be considered silly. The former is but the latter isn't.
>
> You should not fret about your family. Although we love you and worry about your safety, we trust your judgment to follow God's will, and that, after all, is the most important thing for you and for us.
>
> As Grandpa Tuning used to say, "Take your time going, but hurry back."
>
> Love, Noel

With this comforting insight, I left.

EN ROUTE TO AFGHANISTAN

Travel has many added complexities since 9/11. Leaving Portland, Oregon, my journal tells it well:

> "My family: Jeanne, Ted, David, Emily, and Luke saw me off. They waited and watched from a distance as I went through the wanding and searching prior to going to the boarding area. I took off watch, glasses, boots, etc., but still set off alarms. It was my belt buckle! After they finished, I waved at my family and saw Ted vigorously pointing downward. One pant leg was caught on a boot top halfway up my calf. I thought of leaving it that way or, better yet, pulling the other up to make it match!
>
> Thank you so much, friend Ky, (a dear friend) for also coming by and giving me a hug."

On the long flights halfway around the world there are two things I especially enjoy: (1) sitting next to a window and looking at the land we pass over and (2) listening to the fascinating stories of people I sit next to.

This time the journey to London was mostly at night, and cloud cover largely obscured the ground during daylight hours, so I concentrated on the second adventure. I like to pray before a trip, "*Lord, may I be privileged to sit by someone who needs encouraging.*"

My journal reads thus:

> "On the trip from London to Tashkent, Uzbekistan, a man from India, about fifty years of age, sat next to me. He was going home to India for a seven-week visit. He said he did this every year. He had emigrated from India about thirty years previously. Jobs were easy to find then, but many are out of work now. He had worked in a steel mill, as a driver, and lately "in business." I didn't press him for more explanation. He was worried about "the world crisis," with war threatening between Pakistan and India, the lack of work, and the future for his family and children. We talked as best we could, and I separated from him, wishing him well and God's care."

Thank you, Lord, for that interaction. I continue to pray for that man and his family—ones You love exceedingly.

AFGHANISTAN:
"OH MY! WHAT AM I GETTING INTO?"

Our stewardess on this central Asian airline, flying from the capitol to border of Uzbekistan, didn't tell us to fasten our seat belts or put our seatbacks in the full upright position. It wouldn't be possible. Many of the belts would not work, and the seatbacks were in various postures of permanent recline in this small and old Soviet-made airliner.

A few years earlier I would never have believed that I'd be on the other side of the world flying to Afghanistan. Going with medical teams to disasters in other parts of the world and then the events of September 11 changed my thinking. Our intent was to work with the medical problems of a huge refugee population. They are realistically a people who have suffered greatly, impacted by over twenty years of bloody wars.

The loud throb of the plane's ancient prop engines didn't drown out the intense questions I felt inwardly. Would the people of Afghanistan hate me? Would war break out again while I was there? Would I be able truly to help sick and starving people? What about diseases I'd seen little of in my own country? Would I be able to stay healthy? Already I surely missed my wife. Lots of emotions!

I was glad for my traveling partners:

Tom, a very capable emergency care physician. He'd know what to do when we encountered a person who had just lost his or her leg in a land mine explosion, and Michael, an astute diplomat from

South Africa with many connections and ten years of experience in this part of the world. He'd know what to do in politically tense situations.

After flying over rugged, snow-clad mountains, our landing at the border town of Termez was bumpy but safe. Michael informed us we would go to a house in Termez and wait for further permission to cross the Friendship Bridge, which spans the Amu Darya, a large river marking the border between Uzbekistan and Afghanistan. The bridge had been closed for several years and had just recently reopened for the passage of food and a small number of humanitarian workers into Afghanistan.

Termez appeared as a well-kept city, and I especially noted the beautiful clothes of the women. Even those working in a crew along the highway had full-length dresses with most colorful and flowery designs. We noted some areas of new building construction, restaurants and shops that appeared successful, and generally a lack of trash and small but neat yards.

We went to the home of a well-known central Asian trader. His family had connections, including a brother in the capital of Uzbekistan and another who was a prominent general in the Northern Alliance of Afghanistan. Our entry into Afghanistan was only possible with their help. Several men who worked for this family sat around the room. The mood seemed both upbeat and tense. The job of Tom, Michael, and myself was to drink tea, to eat little candies, and to wait.

With some personal relief, I accepted the request to listen in private to the man in charge at this trading station. He'd been having chest pain with typical anginal radiations, seemingly worsening for some time. His blood pressure was high and, indeed, his stress level as well. I shared some of my own personal blood pressure medicine with him, thankful for having it. Concern for his future prompted my giving him added advice, which we in this medical business are always prone to offer.

After about two hours we received word allowing us to proceed onto the Friendship Bridge. This bridge had many military personnel at repeated checkpoints wanting to see our passports, visas, and luggage. It did make me wonder about the name, the Friendship Bridge. It was a slow process. During one long wait I watched the river below. It was an ominous river, probably four hundred yards wide, swirling and running high between reed-enveloped marshes. Bird life seemed absent. The water appeared dark brown, cold with bits of ice, loaded with silt and frequent small trees and sticks. I recalled that I'd been told, "When you return to Uzbekistan, you will think you are in Paris."

We weren't allowed to take a Russian-made jeep with us into Afghanistan because of improper vehicle registration.

While the Uzbek soldiers were finely dressed in neat military garb, on the far side I was impressed by the Afghan soldiers' lack of winter clothing in spite of the bitter cold. It was often mismatched, and they mostly had no more than thin rubbers on their feet. Even so, they waded through snow and mud.

Three fairly new-appearing, dark-windowed cars of a Northern Alliance general met us on the Afghan side and proceeded to carry us across the ever-shifting desert sand toward Mazar-i-Sharif, our destination. Our drivers, by their dodging and racing, obviously had learned their trade while being shot at. The road was totally devoid of signs or lines. Pavement was often broken, and sand dunes were relentlessly competing with shoveling men and children who were trying to clear what road was left. As we sped along, some of the passengers would open the windows a bit and let a bill of Afghan currency swirl behind. There was always a scramble by those shoveling. I wondered if this was their only pay. We passed men and boys and burros carrying loads of brush and weeds cut from scattered parts of this dry land. I imagined that this need for fuel much accelerated the movement of the dunes.

Homes and shops in the few scattered villages were built out of the adobe ground. Ancient vehicles mingled with donkeys and other beasts of burden. Women were covered from the top of their heads to their feet with generally tattered burqas, and the clothes of men and children also often appeared ragged and tinged with the ever-present adobe dust.

Signs of distress impressed us everywhere. Writings on walls indicated land mines were present. Many buildings had been destroyed by shells and bombs. Across the desert sands we saw scattered remnants of destroyed tanks, other armored vehicles, and artillery pieces. I thought that each of these might readily tell some terrible story.

It shouldn't have surprised me that the excitement of the first day in Afghanistan had hardly started. The "rules of the road" dictated that slower-moving traffic should always pull over and let the general's procession, with its constantly beeping horns, get by without slowing its pace. At several checkpoints soldiers hurried to lower the cables crossing the road. As the drivers slowed very little, I wondered several times who would win that race.

Near Mazar-i-Sharif we rapidly approached a little yellow taxi ahead of us. It must have had a driver whose ears had experienced too many explosions at close range. He ignored our rapidly closing in and noisy caravan with horns blaring. The little rusty-yellow taxi was not only packed with people inside but had some hanging on the roof and four in the trunk, with its lid propped up by a stick. The first two cars whipped around it, but, as our driver approached, a large truck loomed in the oncoming lane.

In my mind time seemed to slow abruptly. Thoughts mixed with anxiety. Would our driver choose the truck or the taxi? Was this the way my trip to the other side of the world would end? Too late, he slammed on his brakes, apparently choosing the taxi. I saw the fright on the faces of those hanging on the outside. The peaceful thought that people at home were praying for us passed through my mind. At the last minute our driver cramped his front wheels to the right, and we hurled over a six-foot bank into the desert. The car landed upright and with minimal jolting. Our driver gunned the engine and turned, paralleling the road through the sand. A quarter of a mile farther on a gentler roadside slope again allowed us access to the road, where the other two cars waited. We stopped, and the drivers and passengers piled out, followed by a lot of Afghan hugs, kisses, and backslaps.

Climbing back into our autos, we could see the Hindu Cush Mountains dimly through blowing sand and dust. By then I felt eager to get to my new temporary home. But upon entering Mazar-i-Sharif we drove down narrow, rocky streets to a large adobe-walled house surrounded by men in army uniforms. It was the home of the general. As we got out I was trying to remember, do you cross your heart with your right hand first, before you shake hands, or do you do it afterward?

There had evidently been some radioing ahead, and they were prepared for us. They explained it was their wish to thank Allah that none were killed. A large ram sheep with full curled horns was brought out, wrestled to the ground over a narrow, deep ditch and held by four men as its throat was cut. The sheep tried to kick away its restraints. Blood sprayed in many directions. With some trepidation I again wondered, *What am I getting into?* They then extended an invitation to return that evening and eat the sheep with them.

Loading back into the sedan, our driver hurried us on. It was good to finally get to our Afghan home, with its large steel courtyard doors. We entered and climbed steep steps to where we could stow away our luggage. We found mats on the floor in a cold room. I felt glad I'd come prepared with plenty of long johns, a down sleeping bag, and feather-filled coat—"guaranteed for temperatures well below zero."

That evening we dined with two generals from the Northern Alliance, the trader, and many other men. Only one lady was present, one associated with our medical team. Three representatives from the US government were included. One imposing American carried his machine gun under his long coat and sat at the head of the table with the two generals. During the numerous toasts he spoke in this manner: "We in America are very grateful to you, our Afghan friends, who have fought so hard to rid yourselves of our common enemy. Many of your people have paid the ultimate sacrifice by giving their very lives. Your acts have saved the lives of thousands of my countrymen. For this we are most thankful. We salute you with the highest respect."

The meal was delicious. Small pieces of sheep were impaled, seasoned, and cooked on metal skewers—delicious shish kebabs. Excellent bread and goat cheese, soup, and some fruit were also served. Menservants in their army camouflage uniforms made sure the supply of food and tea never lagged.

After the meal our hosts kindly presented us with small white hats and large thick coats—"Afghan central heating systems." I had not yet learned, as I later did, that at future such gatherings it would be my duty as the eldest there to give the first speech. But I did wonder even more, *Oh my, what am I getting into?* even while appreciating their gracious ways.

SOUNDS IN THE NIGHT

I was glad to see the sky lightening over the Hindu Kush to the southeast. It had been an interrupted night, my first one in Afghanistan. Stray dogs fighting in the street outside our men's sleeping room had jarred me awake several times. I had heard two distant explosions. Traffic began going by on broken pavement early in the morning, even before the official time for lifting of each night's curfew. Trucks slowed for an especially rough area in the street then gunned their engines, briefly drowning out the nearly continuous rhythmic clip-clops of passing burros. There were other puzzling sounds unfamiliar to my ears. In spite of an excellent fleece-lined down sleeping bag placed on two floor mats, longjohn underwear, and heavy socks, my feet failed to warm through most of the night. I had also become aware that one or two of my companions were expert snorers. I determined to find my earplugs and to lay a coat over my feet before another night started.

It was exciting to consider the day ahead, my first day of work in the refugee clinic at Kamer Bandi Balq, "On the Road to Balq." I understood from earlier orientations that it was a smaller camp of only a few thousand refugees, with an excellent chief and little likelihood of danger for us.

My woolen Peruvian-made nightcap was much appreciated as in the dim light I noted locations on the small nearby shelf of the necessities for my dash to the equally frigid squat toilet/bathroom. On it were a washcloth, soap, a small quick-drying towel, shaving cream and safety razor, and toothbrush and paste, with a bottle of water safe to use in washing my face, shaving, and brushing my teeth. Grabbing these things and my glasses, pulling on my trousers, and slipping into my shower slippers, the cold air and nature propelled me quickly toward the bathroom. *(I hate squat toilets. I always have visions of falling in.)*

Others were beginning to rouse as I returned to the men's sleeping room. They would be close behind me. Having finished my morning ablutions, I added a shot of Right Guard under each arm, put on warmer clothes, and began fumbling at starting the stove. It was a simply made contrivance with a tank holding about a gallon of diesel. An adjustable valve dripped fuel into a line feeding the bottom of a circular burning chamber. This firebox was about ten inches across and sixteen inches high. A small stovepipe, which leaked soot into our room, extended to the ceiling. Under this entire contrivance a large metal pan separated the stove from the floor and hopefully added some safety. (I soon learned that the two teams before us had fire flare outside of the stove on three different occasions. It had become policy never to leave one burning unless someone was in the room.) I started the diesel drip and opened the top of the stove. Several matches later, a fire flared up from the bowels of the firebox. The air gradually warmed (for at least two feet) in all directions.

The house in which we were billeted was owned by a general of the Northern Alliance, the same benefactor who had helped us get access to Afghanistan. Our rooms for sleeping and eating were on the top floor of this three-story building. Even though it was little heated, had only erratic electricity from a small generator purchased by Medical Teams International, and had no phone lines, it did have intermittent running water and some blue paint on its exterior. It was far superior to most homes in Mazar-i-Sharif. A small open-air balcony-like passageway on the south side of this floor connected our sleeping room to the kitchen and eating area.

As I crossed that open area I couldn't help but pause to view the impressive ramparts of the Hindu Kush Mountains looming to the south. The blowing sand had mostly obscured them the day before. It was a rugged range of mountains. Snow extended from the high peaks to near the edge of the desert at its feet. No timber appeared in the valleys between crags, such as we would expect at home. I thought, *This sight would certainly stir a mountain climber's heart!*

Briefly I noted the surrounding buildings, adobe or brick-walled, with adobe roofs. Some roofs had grown grass in warmer weather, now dry and yellowed. High adobe walls enclosed the small backyards of many. A few thin lines of smoke ascended from some of the houses to mingle in a slight haze. To my right rose the walls of an ancient fortress with eroding gun emplacements showing the effects of time and weather.

In a small yard about a hundred feet distant, a man, turbaned and with a thick coat, paced back and forth. Mud clung to his shoes. A rifle was slung over one shoulder. He occasionally glanced my way. I remember thinking, *This is Afghanistan; I hope our bombers haven't destroyed some of his family.*

Hurrying on to the eating area, I passed through a small enclosed room at the top of the stairs with its long row of outdoor shoes, including my own fleece-lined boots. Opening the door to the eating area, I viewed an old table with chairs for about eight people. At the opposite end of the room was a long red and purple sofa. It had bunny rabbit designs but was also very worn, appeared to have "severe scoliosis (a badly bent back) and was near terminal."

Close by was a small diesel stove, a replica of the one in the men's sleeping room. And it was cold! Although I could hear stirrings from the kitchen I was the first to the dining area and so the ritual was repeated: diesel started—drip, drip, many matches—scratch, scratch … and finally a burst of flame. It would make a good place to huddle.

Hamayoun, our cook, entered the room quietly with his stack of freshly baked bread and two thermos pitchers, one with hot tea and the other with hot water. We greeted each other with "Salaam a lakum," and "w lakum a salaam," and with our right hands quickly crossed our hearts and then shook hands. I was learning. I liked the sparkle in his eyes. He was a smiler and was eager to help me in my fumbling. His English was as nonexistent as my Dari, so we had fun trying to understand each other, and considerable reason to smile.

He returned to the kitchen to get some goat cheese, a butter-like spread, marmalade, and chunky peanut butter. Others of our group were quickly appearing, and after greetings and chuckling over the previous day's events, we seated ourselves and someone prayed our meal's grace.

The fresh bread, formed into rolls about an inch thick, circular and about six inches across, was lightly browned and had a chewy crust. It was as delicious as its fragrance. These rolls continued to be breakfast fare each day for my two months in Afghanistan, and I never tired of them. The hot tea was just right for cold mornings, and instant coffee was available to mix with the hot water. We took care to use either bottled water or water that had been boiled for nearly twenty minutes. A sign on the door to the eating room reading "Ye Olde Barn Door" had been placed by someone who evidently hoped to add to the room's warmth.

Dr. Neil, a pediatrician from Portland, Oregon, and part of the previous team, was our leader. As we ate he apprised us further of the camps that were our responsibility, Kamer Bandi Balq and Korazon II. In addition, we were to make rounds with the Afghani doctors at the Civilian Hospital, also called the Public Health Hospital, in Mazar-i-Sharif. Kamer Bandi Balq was a small and a considered-to-be-safe camp, while Korazon II was quite different. It was a large refugee camp of about thirty thousand people, erected in some open spaces in the northern part of Mazar. It was considered at that time to be an unsafe camp for us Americans to enter. Numerous Taliban had defected or melted into the populace as their fortunes had crumbled only a short time previously. To some it would have been an honorable thing to kill "their enemy." On the edge of this massive refugee camp MTI had rented an adobe house with two rooms, barren except for a small stove in one. It had a large walled yard with a strong gate. Guards manned the entry, and a police station was close by.

We were also told about many meetings sponsored by the United Nations, where attendance was expected. Of special importance were the security meetings, where all the nongovernmental organizations (NGOs) met together with United Nations personnel weekly or oftener to assess rumors and realities having to do with safety. All of these things were discussed and assignments were passed out. (Later, in 2011, this facility was bombed by the Taliban, and many died.)

In this area, with a population of probably just over a million people, were just four hospitals: the Civilian Hospital and a Military Hospital in Mazar-i-Sharif, a small hospital at Koudebarq (about twenty kilometers to the west), and the Jordanian Hospital, set up near the previously bombed-out airport to the east of Mazar. We were told it had excellent doctors from Jordan and was also well equipped and very useful as a referral center. The Afghan hospitals, having suffered through years of war, had little left with which to work.

Dr. Buist decided that Dr. Tom and I, being new, would go with him to meet the doctors at the Civilian Hospital. Dr. Bill from Seattle and Tom and Donna Armstrong from southern Washington State, along with three Afghan doctors, went on to the refugee camps. Tom is an EMT-firefighter and Donna is an RN. At that time the three young Afghan doctors working with us were Dr. Abdullah, a surgeon; Dr. Zabi, a pediatrician; and Dr. Nadia, a lady internist. We were also informed that it would be needful at some future time to meet physicians at the other hospitals.

Leaving the breakfast room to pick up what was needed for the day, I made sure the "barn door" was well closed. As I passed along the open porch area, three white doves on a nearby rooftop cooed and strutted—*reassurance*. After collecting some medical gear, then putting on my wool-lined boots, I descended a cement staircase to the courtyard area with its high walls. There, it was a privilege to greet all of those who would help us so very much: the doctors, our guards, translators, and drivers. They seemed a pleasant group of workers. Contrary to most Afghani men, these were mostly clean-shaven or had only small moustaches. I wondered what tragic memories might be hiding behind their warm greetings. The physicians all spoke some English, and I knew I'd learn much from them. It became apparent that it was proper to call each doctor by his or her first name: Dr. Bill, Dr. Nadia, Dr. Abdullah, etc.

Greetings were exchanged in Dari, the common local language, and English, along with the ritual hand movements and handshakes.

I recalled in my mind, "We want to help where possible, but we also want to learn from you." This was our approach to the physicians in Afghanistan, and it is very realistic. I am confident the Afghan physicians appreciate it.

Our van proceeded out of the large steel gates past Islamadin, a tall, regal, Afghani gentleman who served as our most capable commander of the guards. Under a small-billed cap he had a slight smile and returned my wave. Although the guards were not supposed to be armed, I wondered about the bulge under his thick coat near his right arm. The solid steel gates closed behind as we entered the world of broken pavement and varied vehicles, animals, and pedestrians. Traffic flowed in a seemingly totally chaotic fashion. About five hundred meters to the west our van entered a very busy intersection. A policeman stood in the middle of it with his baton in one hand waving vigorously this way and that. It was not apparent to my inexperienced eye that anyone was paying attention to his waves or his whistles. Our driver found an opening, or someone he could bluff, and quickly dodged behind the traffic officer onto the strand of pavement going southward. The lines of traffic going in the same direction varied from two to four vehicles wide. There were no street or lane markings of any type. A parallel lane on the other side of the garbage-covered median seemed to be proceeding northward in an equally disorganized manner—*It seemed every man, boy, horse, or donkey for himself.*

Lining this moving mass were carts with various wares—such as aged pots and pans—interspersed with areas of ground displaying ancient car parts on a sheet of plastic. About two hundred meters down this muddy boulevard we suddenly turned into a narrow, congested lane between two small buildings and stopped. Two soldiers clad in turbans, military jackets, baggy Afghan trousers, and mud-covered rubbers peered into our van's windows from both sides. Our driver talked rapidly to these serious, rifle-bearing guards, and we were waved on. Beneath cold and overcast skies we entered the driveway to the Civilian or Public Health Hospital of Mazar-i-Sharif.

As we parked in a large and crowded courtyard, many faces turned toward us. Indeed we were the strangers. I looked for a friendly face, a smile. There were none. Expressions seemed to show only bitterness and suffering. I thought, *Hades must seem like this.*

With some trepidation and no alternative, I moved with my companions toward a large crowd of men waiting in an emergency area. Some were squatting near a wall while others who were standing pressed toward the steps leading to the men's emergency entrance. A guard with his rifle would periodically pull aside a worn and dirty rug that covered the doorway, letting another man through. One man on the steps was shouting at the guard. Through the thick crowd I heard the guard's loud and brief response, and saw it accompanied by a poke from the rifle butt.

In another area women clad in their ever-present burqas crowded toward a doorway. Across the courtyard we saw parents with waiting children. Our interpreter called out to the guard, and we were motioned toward the door and on through. Dr. Neil told us the hospital director's office was nearby.

After explaining who we were, our interpreter inquired of a man at an inside desk if it would be possible to see the hospital administrator, Dr. Rahbi. We did not have long to wait before being ushered into his office. It was a small room, simply furnished, with his brown desk just in front of a plain curtain covering an outside window. Papers on his desk were more neatly arranged than mine at home. The three remaining sides of the small sitting area had low covered couches with worn upholstery surrounding a small central coffee table. While standing we introduced ourselves to Dr. Rahbi and others there and told them briefly of our mission: "To help with health care in any way that we might, and to learn from them." Dr. Rahbi motioned for us to be seated and spoke a few words to an aide. A small dish of paper-covered candies and tiny cups of tea were brought. He expressed, "We have been surveyed by several groups, but from it, not much help has materialized," and "Things in the countryside are only growing worse." Their hospital was seeing five hundred to eight hundred people daily. They had very little equipment. In fact, they related, "There is only one blood pressure cuff in the hospital and very few stethoscopes." We told him that we had a few extra and would aim to bring them to him soon. Dr. Rahbi further informed us that they had been given a new ultrasound machine but didn't know about setting it up. It was not yet unpacked. Dr. Tom was experienced in doing and teaching ultrasound, and we arranged that he would return on Saturday to help set up the machine and start teaching its use. He would also bring some blood pressure cuffs. Together we would return the following Tuesday morning to make rounds with the doctors on the internal medicine service. As we left and climbed back in our van, we felt some sense of progress.

KAMER BANDI BALQ—BROWN DRINKING WATER

Traveling northwest out of Mazar-i-Sharif, our van passed slowly between a colorful array of waiting buggy-like vehicles, each with a single horse and driver. These horse-drawn taxis generally had two wooden wheels with iron rims, two seats, a high foldable top, and a trace up each side of the horse attached to its harness. Red, yellow, blue, and green fluffy balls, tassels, and plumes decorated the horses and buggies. These seemed to be mostly made of yarn. Tiny bells were included on some of the waiting conveyances. I wondered, *Would the Taliban have allowed such a gaudy display?* The thought crossed my mind, *I must take a ride in one someday.*

A bit farther on we saw large groups of people—men, women, and children—along the road. Some had carts, some traveled with burros, but all hurried in a single direction. Our driver frequently used his horn, slowed, and then sped up again. As the throng became very dense the object of their intensity became apparent, a United Nations Food Distribution Center. Giving food to such a large and hardly manageable mass appeared to us a daunting task. Would there be plenty for all?

We passed by a large open area about the size of two football fields with high adobe walls. It was filled with cattle, camels, burros, sheep, and goats. Our interpreter explained that this was the market where these animals were bought and sold. It looked like an active place. We saw only men and boys herding and caring for the animals.

Remains of armored vehicles and artillery pieces were common. In one place we observed many destroyed vehicles that had been heaped together. Ruins of buildings were everywhere. There must have been some intense fighting on this edge of Mazar.

Soon small fields emerged between clusters of adobe houses. Most were encircled by modest mud fences about a meter and a half high. Our driver abruptly slowed and turned into one of these areas. Dr. Bill told us that this was Kamer Bandi Balq.

The alley into the refugee camp was totally unimproved. It was narrow with a surface of slick adobe mud. Two young boys stood watching as we started down the roadway. The larger one wore a dark coat, too big for him, and the smaller a tiny reddish jacket. Their typical baggy trousers were muddy up to the knees. The older boy, probably about seven, smiled shyly and put his arm around the younger. I imagined they were brothers. On our left were brown adobe walls and on our right deep pits from which the building material had been excavated. I was glad our van had four-wheel-drive and that our driver proceeded with some caution.

About two hundred meters down this roadway we abruptly entered into a more open area, and the camp and its people became evident. To our right, crowded, small, homemade tents left little unoccupied space over several acres. Opposite, about fifty people crowded near a small adobe building, waiting for our arrival. The village chief emerged from this group and greeted us. He was a little taller than most Afghan men, had a full beard with streaks of gray, and wore a turban and the usual Afghan clothing of loose, baggy trousers and a long thick coat. He looked like a man to be respected. Those around him certainly seemed to acknowledge his leadership but not in a fearful manner.

Earlier that day word had come asking us to also survey the situation of a small hospital at Hyroton, some sixty miles away near the Friendship Bridge. We decided then that Dr. Bill and I would go there with Michael while Dr. Neil and Dr. Tom would stay and work with the Afghan doctors in the small clinic at Kamer Bandi Balq. Before leaving, Bill and I had an opportunity to look around the refugee camp. Three of us, along with Dr. Neil and the chief, walked over to look at the encampment. An entourage, curious about these Westerners, followed. (Dr. Neil is a very tall man, and this always added to his large audience.) Tents were closely spaced with central poles holding up a variety of roofs composed of stretched gunnysacks, plastic sheets, or blankets. Generally, one end was closed, and a glance into the open end revealed some bedding and a few personal belongings. Usually a pot was near that opening with coals underneath from a fire of weeds or twigs that had been burnt for cooking. A few stones were in place to hold the pot above the heat. Many tents appeared empty. The chief said there were only about 350 refugees now living in the camp. Most of the original two thousand or so had been assimilated into surrounding villages but still returned here to get food distribution and to attend the clinic when needed. The United Nations was strongly encouraging and implementing their return to their villages.

Dr. Neil and the chief showed us how the water source had been improved. NWMTI had purchased several large, clean, metal barrels for drinking water. Each had a large lid on top and a spigot at the bottom. We looked inside one, and indeed the water did appear clean. Our organization was providing a stipend for owners of burros to go a considerable distance to a well and bring back clean water. Even as we talked, a young man walked up leading his burro loaded with full water cans hanging on both sides. Dr. Neil inquired to make sure that this duty was being shared by several. The stipend would be very helpful to a family without income.

We followed a winding pathway along narrow adobe ridges between pits, from which adobe building material had been dug, to a small irrigation ditch some two hundred meters away. It ran brown with dirty water. This had been the camp's previous source of drinking water. About ten people had died in the camp from gastrointestinal disease in recent weeks. Clean water would greatly reduce this mortality rate, mostly affecting the very young and the old.

In a small field nearby about twenty fat-tailed sheep were guarded by a lad, and a bit further away a team of oxen was plowing a small field. We detoured briefly to watch. The plow was a wooden one, crudely made with a single handle that simply dug a furrow in the surface of the ground without turning the sod as a metal plow might. Another Afghan man had a bucket and was sowing wheat, throwing it with his hand where the soil was loosened. The burlap bag from which he was taking seed had English words stating that the grain was treated with a fungicide and was poisonous for human consumption. We hoped that someone was telling the Afghan people the meaning of these foreign words.

On returning to the clinic area they showed us a small courtyard surrounded by its adobe fence with a rope across the center about two meters off the ground. This was the volleyball court. What a great idea. But it was also a private area with many piles of human feces along the inside of the fence. The refugees had no toilet facilities and had to make-do. My thoughts included, *A volleyball game here might have its complications*, and, *yes, indeed, Afghanistan is a land of large contrasts, magnified by its years of tragedy.*

It was noon and time for Dr. Bill and me to return with our driver to our house in Mazar preparatory to the afternoon inspection of the distant hospital at Hyroton.

On subsequent days I was able to return and work in the clinic at Kamer-Bandi-Balq several times. There are things I particularly recall. One day while working with my interpreter, Amanolla, I saw several young children, one after the other. It seemed that each one took a look at me and burst out crying—unless he or she was too ill to cry. I thought, *Now if I just had a long beard and some different clothes, perhaps these little ones would be less fearful.*" It was cold, and respiratory infections were common.

My journal states, "I saw a lot of people of all ages. It is surprising how well many have fared generally, in spite of dreadful living conditions. One little guy looked pretty wasted. His stomach was big, and his muscles were very small. His mother reported that he was having 'meat in his bowels.' On further inquiry it was apparent that this was a worm infestation as well as malnutrition. We treated him with Mbendizol (a worm medicine) and multivitamins."

As I greeted and shook hands with some of the men, I was aware that their hands seemed warmer than mine. They had found the secret of gathering warmth by crouching on the sunny side of a wall. A pan of coals, from tiny limbs of brush collected on nearby hills, was commonly brought by. I was thankful to warm my hands.

In asking the chief what else the camp needed, he expressed the wish to have some large teapots for boiling water. Subsequently I did find four in Mazar-e-Sharif that would hold about five gallons each and delivered them. The chief rewarded my efforts with a large Afghan hug.

HYROTON HOSPITAL— MIXING HOPE AND DEEP CONCERN

The road across the desert to the Friendship Bridge had not improved from the day before. The same gusting wind was giving life to the lurking dunes. Again we sped past burros and turbaned men and boys carrying immense loads of brush.

Pulling into a narrow driveway by a large but dilapidated adobe building, we were told that this was the Hyroton Hospital. A young Afghan doctor met us. Through two interpreters Michael explained our mission. Our host was most courteous in showing us around in great detail. What appeared to have once been a very adequate small hospital had deteriorated into a destitute clinic, but obviously it was better than nothing for the thousands of people living in this area near the border of Uzbekistan. Some of the roof was caving in. Little heat was available to help patients endure the late January weather. Checking hydrants for water produced few that worked, and we were told that it was unsafe for drinking. The bathroom, with its squat toilet and a filthy tub, was most odiferous. No lab work had been possible "since the Taliban came." In spite of this, three doctors did the best they could with the remnants. They were seeing about 100 to 150 patients a day. One slept there each night waiting for emergencies. An ancient operating room table was used for minor procedures and had an unemptied bucket of bloody sponges beside it. According to the young physician, attempts to transport seriously ill patients over unreliable roads the fifty miles to Mazar-i-Sharif often ended with patients dying en route. The face and manner of this Afghan physician spoke distinct concern mixed with hope for a better future. It all tugged at our hearts.

Dr. Bill and I generated a report for United Nations information.

A FOCUS OF RECENT HISTORY: STEPPING CAREFULLY

We in America had heard about the uprising and tragedy that enveloped an old fortress being used as a prison some fifteen or twenty kilometers west of Mazar-i Sharif. Not only had many hundreds of Taliban and Northern Alliance soldiers died, but it was here that the first American, Johnny Spann, was killed during the war in Afghanistan, and a wounded John Walker Lindh was found as the fighting reached its bloody conclusion.

Friday was our "day off." In the Muslim culture of Afghanistan it was a day of rest and not appropriate to attempt to work, although some of the shops were open in Mazar. Michael suggested we visit that old fortress, Qala-i-Jangi. Mukhabat, a young lady from Uzbekistan who was now also working for MTI, had been there as a reporter for the *Los Angeles Times* during the terrible fight. She would accompany us.

We traveled west of Mazar city, past small villages and irrigated farmland with now mostly small barren fields. Abruptly the walls of Qala-i-Jangi loomed to the south. I was amazed by the enormity of this old fortress. Its ramparts were at least twenty meters high, built of thick adobe blocks with a steep earthen base supporting the lower half. These walls stretched irregularly for four hundred meters or so on each of its four sides. Machine gun and artillery emplacements were located uppermost at intervals of perhaps a hundred meters. As we took a slightly winding roadway toward the ancient fortress, bullet pockmarks from the fierce fighting became evident in its walls. Near the northeast corner a huge gap appeared in the upper half of the bulwark.

Our road circled the east side of the fortress and then joined another road from the south as it turned toward the huge main gate at the southeast corner. It was well guarded by eight soldiers bearing rifles, machine guns and rocket launchers. An armored vehicle waited nearby. The soldiers' faces were grim. Several appeared to be little more than children. I was thankful for Michael and Mukhabat, who were on good terms with the generals of the Northern Alliance. Michael conversed with the soldiers a bit, a call was made on a handheld radio into the inner sanctum, the gate was opened, and we were briskly waved through.

Huge residuals of the recent carnage were all about us as our van made its way along the road leading toward the fort's headquarters: trees shredded and broken, fragmented remnants of walls and buildings, demolished vehicles, and the inside of the fortress wall was scarred by thousands of bullets. By contrast, the headquarters building had already been mostly rebuilt. Its walls had been repaired and freshly painted. A small porch had an obviously new iron railing.

Michael informed us that the commander we would be seeing was one of General Dostum's main subgenerals. As we stopped nearby a handsome guard came to meet us. Contrary to the soldiers at the main gate with their varied combinations of ill-fitting military and civilian garb, he appeared trim with camouflage hat and trousers, neat boots, and a heavy greenish-blue parka that extended to his thighs. He had thick black eyebrows, a trim mustache, and a pleasant and confident smile. Under his left arm he carried a large-caliber machine gun with its tripod. He and Michael exchanged greetings, and we were told that the general was waiting to see us. With this we dismounted and were ushered through a shiny new wooden door.

The reception room gave no hint of the remains of terror that lay outside the door. Michael and the general met with greetings, warm embraces, and kisses to the side of each others' face. Two Afghan aides were present also, and we greeted the general and the aides with "Salaam a Lakum," our right hands over our hearts and firm handshakes. The general was a squarely built man who looked neat in his light brown military garb with red epaulets. His smile was warm, almost shy. I wondered how he dealt with his memories.

As we were being seated on comfortable couches I glanced around the room. Freshly painted on one wall was a large mural showing mountains with rugged crags and slopes with areas of trees both near and distant. A beautiful blue river flowed through the valley. Wildflowers adorned some hillsides.

Aides served us tea and candies while Michael and the general conversed. As their dialogue was interpreted we learned more of the terrible fight. The general had been on the fortress wall near the present breach. A stray American bomb, the only one that had gone awry, hit near him, destroying a tank of the Northern Alliance with its five occupants. He related that since that blast he had been unable to hear well. We offered to look in his ears. Dr. Bill took my otoscope and found what we expected—both eardrums were perforated. We sadly informed him of the problem and that we had nothing that could heal his hearing. He did not seem surprised.

We were offered a guided tour of the destruction. Several soldiers accompanied us. The pathway led past remnants of a large rose garden showing attempts at restoration with evidence of some recent trimming and cultivation. (I recalled that the dead are generally buried within a day in this culture and the wondering thought crossed my mind if some might be under this newly cultivated area. I did not ask.) We followed the pathway on between two large buildings, partially demolished, and into a yard the size of two football fields. There we saw almost total destruction. Hundreds of captured Taliban were brought here as the Northern Alliance, with support from American warplanes, rapidly regained control of Northern Afghanistan. Apparently many prisoners had hidden weaponry and revolted against their captors soon after their arrival. The remains of the ordnance depot they had captured lay just to our right. Ahead about forty meters a few walls and rooms of the building where John Walker Lindh had hidden were still standing. To the left was a long row of low buildings that had stabled horses for the fortress. They were now empty.

As we followed our guides around the ruins of the central building we noted both spent and active ordnance littering the ground. Some lay in heaps and in other places was spread like gravel. I was careful to place my feet where footprints were already evident. This building had large and complex subterranean rooms and passageways. We were told that here Lindh and others refused to give up as the fighting wound down and only came out when it was flooded with water. After privately playing a game of "double dare you" with myself, Dr. Tom and I crawled through a hole in the top of the basement wall. With a flashlight we carefully descended. It was yet very wet, and the remains of garments covered much of the immediate floor space. Realizing the lack of safety, we did not explore far.

One of the soldiers accompanying us told of being a Northern Alliance guard during this tragedy. Early in the uprising he had been captured, bound, and placed in a ground-level room in this same building. He showed us where he had been left trussed and unable to move during the fighting. Fortunately, the wall he had lain against was yet standing.

Three trucks the prisoners had commandeered were only about thirty meters to the west. They were twisted heaps of metal and wood.

Mukhabet showed us the high fortress wall to the east behind which she had hidden. She related that several members of the American Special Forces were on that wall, watching and calling in air strikes. Soldiers of the Northern Alliance would advance on the enemy for a bit amid much fierce fighting, then alternately retreat to the walls to allow bombs to be dropped by the planes overhead. She told of seeing a group of Taliban fighters trying to escape over that same wall. They were caught, and their throats were cut. The total experience was described as "horrible."

Nearly three months later I was privileged to revisit the site of all this carnage. Much had been done in cleaning up the devastation.

The breach in the wall was mostly repaired, live and spent ordinance had been gathered into piles—though some small bullets, shells, and slugs were still evident mixed with the gravel, and the rose garden was blooming. Most of the roses were dark red.

KHORASAN "UNSAFE"

Writing about my patients in Afghanistan is difficult. I feel the stirring of deep emotions. The many limitations in diagnosis and treatment, the difficulties in follow-up, and the extreme hardship of their daily lives still profoundly influence my thoughts and feelings.

I had read and heard a great deal about the refugee camp Khorasan prior to arriving there. It was a camp of some thirty thousand displaced people on the northern side of Mazar-i-Sharif. My first morning there had been only a powdering of new snow. It was rapidly melting, leaving mud. Our van wound through those muddy streets lined by mostly one-story adobe houses pressed together. Some streets had been graded and graveled, others were totally unimproved. There were no names on the street corners or numbers on buildings. I wondered how our driver knew exactly where to turn and which of the thousands of lowly homes was the place to stop and pick up Dr. Nadia. She was waiting. A single jumpseat, slightly separated from the others, had been left for her. As she seated herself, she pulled the light blue burqa away from her face and greeted us all with a beautiful smile and "Good morning."

We passed a well where people pumped water by hand. Most were young boys with buckets often carried on both ends of a wooden shoulder yoke. Nearby was a school with high walls and a narrow gate. We could see no activity there. A bit farther, on our left, appeared an extensive field covered with thousands of small pup tents. In each, the supporting structure of a central timber was similar, but the roofs were quite varied: canvas, blankets, rugs, plastic, and burlap were included. Some people moved about, but most squatted on the muddy ground by their tents or just stood and stared. Smoke here and there curled up from the tiny tents. This was Khorasan.

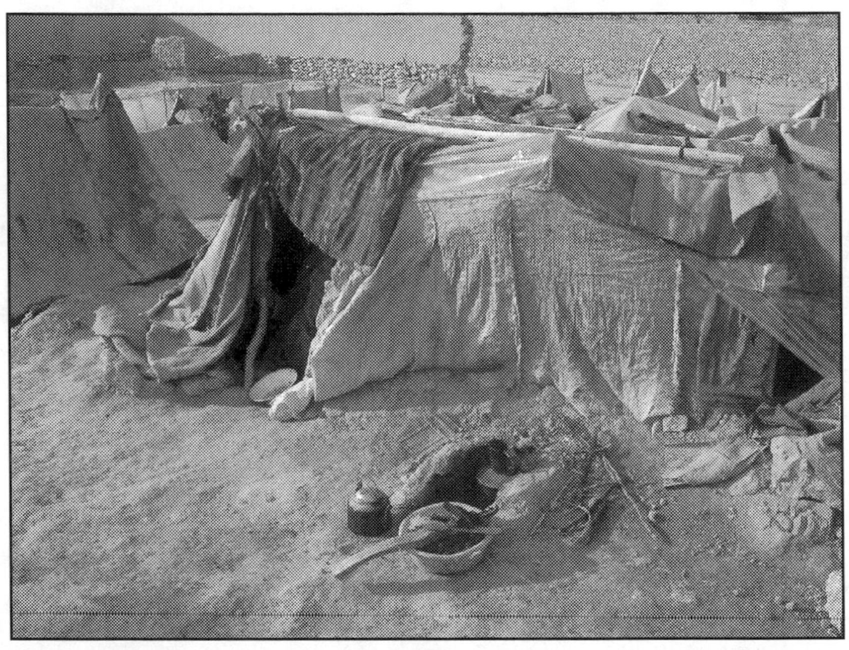

A crowd had gathered near the end of a lane, pushing toward a heavy wooden gate in a whitewashed wall. It encircled the rented building to be used as our clinic. Burqas covered the faces and figures of all the women. Probably a third of the adults were men, generally turbaned and wearing a variety of coats and blankets. Many men and women carried small children while older children stood among them.

I saw much urgency, some jostling, and no smiling. Nearly a hundred people were in the group. Others were approaching.

Our driver pointed toward the gate as we disembarked, and we were told to stay close behind. Pressing through the crowd, I remembered with a bit of apprehension that I was the stranger and we'd been told to regard it as an "unsafe camp." My thoughts quickly changed as I saw the faces of children, many of whom were obviously ill. Some of the adults reaching toward us seemed to be calling out for help. Though I couldn't understand Dari these sights and sounds certainly connected. I was deeply stirred.

Marian, the gatekeeper, opened it just enough to let us through with our packs, medicine chest, and red folding chairs; then, shouting at the crowd, she pushed the gate closed. Marian had been the gatekeeper since the clinic had opened only a few weeks before. Although occasionally she required other help, for the most part she was the main person keeping order. I was told that she often "patted down" women in their burqas. We wondered if that was really needed.

Crossing a small yard, our group entered the two-room house rented for a clinic. Thick walls, ceiling, and floor were adobe. One room had a tiny diesel-burning stove. It added a little warmth. A wooden cot was in the far end of that same room. We stretched a wire and hung a small plastic tarp to make it a private place where patients needing some disrobing could be taken. Three groupings of two or three of the red plastic chairs were arranged in the two rooms; the large metal medicine chest was placed centrally, and we were ready for business.

Dr. Abdullah is a young Afghan surgeon who Northwest Medical Teams hired to work with us. He not only spoke his native tongue but was fluent in English, as are many of the Afghan doctors. It was my privilege to work with him initially. Later I would work separately using an interpreter. Our first patients were promptly let in through the courtyard gate, and three were brought to our room.

Dr. Abdullah spoke to a mother hidden in a dirty, worn burqa and carrying a small girl, probably about two years old. As she approached, the child demonstrated a weak, raspy cough. We learned the little girl had been coughing for about a week and was becoming listless and eating poorly. Indeed she appeared quite ill, with drawn face and increased warmth to the touch. However, her mouth was moist, and other markers of hydration seemed normal. Breathing was a bit rapid but not labored. As we removed her outer coat then sneaked our cold stethoscopes down the back and front of her thin dress she squirmed and tried to pull away. A large area of congestion was apparent in her right lower lung area. She had pneumonia. After mixing clean water in a bottle of antibiotic powder, Dr. Abdulla showed the mother how to shake the bottle and then pour it into a tiny plastic teaspoon. It was to be given three times daily. Like most of the refugees, this woman was illiterate. He marked a tiny instruction sheet that showed a rising sun, a midday sun, and setting sun and told her the meaning—one teaspoon full of antibiotic three times a day. Again he made sure the mother knew to shake up the suspension each time before giving it. We were hopeful this little one would soon be well, but the mother was told to bring her back if worse or not soon better. We hoped she understood. The mother, with her burqa now pulled away from her face, seemed grateful.

During this day and subsequent wintry days in this huge camp, we were to see numerous children and adults with pneumonia. One morning as we arrived, Dr. Zabi rushed out to meet us holding a tiny boy, who appeared only about a year old and had been breathing with great difficulty. The tiny child had just stopped breathing, and Dr. Zabi was giving mouth to mouth resuscitation while holding the infant in his arms. He and the extremely worried mother were quickly loaded into the van and disappeared toward the Civilian Hospital with the doctor yet breathing with force into the tiny boy's mouth. This little one lived.

Another lady wore a very dirty light-blue burqa. I understood why it had not been washed for a long time. As she pulled it back from her face I saw a lady who appeared much older than her forty years. She was thin and wrinkled. When asked, "What is your problem?" my translator replied, "She has a cold—for about a year." This response, of course, raised red flags. She was coughing up sputum that was not bloody but was described as thick, green and profuse. Night sweats were usual. I listened with my stethoscope. Her left lung had congestion throughout, with varied sounds that told me much. Of course I suspected pulmonary tuberculosis, but did start a course of antibiotics for pneumonia and arranged for a chest x-ray to be done at the Civilian Hospital. Sputum cultures and microscopic views were not available. She was to return with the x-rays, which is standard procedure there. If the probability of TB was confirmed, we would transfer her care to an NGO (nongovernment organization) that focused on the long-term care of tuberculosis patients.

We saw tuberculosis in all its forms. Later that day I saw a patient with a tender abdomen. It was swollen, and intra-abdominal fluid was evident on exam. His abdomen felt doughy to palpation. I recalled patients from my past. This consistency is highly suggestive of TB inside the abdominal cavity. Again that day a young man presented with swollen lymph nodes in his neck. They were only moderately firm and minimally tender. They had been slowly increasing over a period of several months, and a little inflammation could now be seen. He had no symptoms of mouth or throat or lung problems by his history or my inspection, but was having night sweats. Again I felt this was likely tuberculosis. Even though Dr. Abdullah easily could have done a biopsy of the neck lumps, there was no pathologist to inspect the biopsy specimen with a microscope or method for growing TB germs in this part of Afghanistan. Once again we had to do what was possible, and embarked on a course of antibiotic treatment for TB. This treatment needed to last for many months, and we hoped the before-mentioned NGO would be able to follow up on what we started. I would surely like to know how this turned out.

One arriving patient walked to a folding chair in our waiting room with difficulty. Her breathing was labored, and near her ankles I could see badly swollen legs. She had been increasingly more short of breath for several months. To be able to breathe at night, she was now having to prop herself up with what meager belongings she and her children could stack together in their tiny tent. Her husband had died in the war.

As was appropriate in this culture, a female friend accompanied her as Dr. Abdullah and I went behind the blue drape and into the privacy of the end of our room with its wooden table. With my stethoscope I could hear abnormal moisture in her lungs about halfway up on both sides. Tapping over the bases of both lungs with my fingers produced the abnormal dullness of dense fluid accumulation. With each rapid beat of her struggling heart, I could hear the sounds of a leaking heart valve. There were near 160 beats a minute, about twice a normal rate. Her severe swelling reached up the entire length of both legs. This thirty-year-old lady was obviously in congestive heart failure and would die soon.

Using medications to help her kidneys get rid of the huge fluid overload and to strengthen her heart, I hoped she might live. A week later she was feeling much better, had lost her leg swelling, and her lungs were almost clear. On further follow-up, two weeks afterward, she was doing even better and informed me that she was going back to her own village. I made sure she knew what medications she was taking, and my translator wrote out in detail dosages and frequency of medications. We hoped she would some way be able to buy more. Even though medicines can be purchased without a prescription in Afghanistan, the realities are that pharmacies may be distant and that you have no money! I have often wondered what became of this young widow and her children.

Gastroenteritis was common even though the weather was cold. This was part of each clinic day. Can you imagine walking through a portion of this huge encampment where there had been no toilets, and people squatting either inside their tiny tent or on the adobe mud nearby? Thankfully Tom, the emergency medical technician/firefighter working with us, had arranged for several toilet pits with screens around them to be built within the camp. He had hired several Afghan men. This would help.

I especially remember a slight-of-build thirteen-year-old girl in a ragged dress and heavy jacket. She did not look up while trying to pull away from her father, who had a firm grip on her wrist. He father explained that a few years before, the girl had been alone in their house when a fierce battle broke out, with the house caught between warring parties. She had never been the same since—was continually trying to run away from home, even at night, and had regressed in her learning. She now was not able to count or read. I asked Dr. Neil, a superb pediatrician with MTI, for his thoughts. He talked at length with the father. There being no psychiatric help in that part of Afghanistan, our suggestions were limited. Even as we talked, the girl sneaked away and hurried toward the outer gate.

"He (or she) is sad" was often a large component of the illnesses we saw that day in Afghanistan. And many times in the weeks that followed. What to do? Were our efforts like throwing tiny pebbles into the ocean? Only God knows.

My journal records other patients that especially impressed me: "a lactating mother with a large breast abscess with dying tissue, a boy with a severe sore by his anus, a lady with terrible untreated rheumatoid arthritis for four years, a boy with difficult burns—being cleaned and treated with Silvadene creme, dressings applied, etc."

I had brought a lot of "whirligigs" with me from America. They were made of firm cardboard discs with a circle of string going through on either side of the center. As we left after our day's work, I tried to show some of the children just outside our clinic gate how to twirl them to wind the string up, then to gently pull and release to unwind and rewind the little discs. Like kids everywhere, they tended to pull too vigorously but gradually learned and made them hum! However, there soon gathered a totally uncontrolled crowd of children. I learned the necessity to do such things in a more private setting, one child at a time. It was fun.

That evening we took a tiny baby with a cleft lip and palate, and a lady with abdominal pain, to the Jordanian Hospital near the previously bombed-out airport of Mazar-e-Sharif. This hospital had been flown in with much American help and had highly qualified medical personnel and excellent equipment. Security was tight, and indeed many people were being stopped, questioned, and searched at about four separate checkpoints. I'm sure that many were never allowed near the hospital.

At each checkpoint, our situation was explained by Dr. Nadia with surprisingly forceful voice and motions. We journeyed past the wreckage of houses, several armored vehicles, and MiGs on the airport's border. At the last checkpoint all the Afghan helpers and patients had to get out of the van and were searched or gone over with wands. I showed them my identification and was motioned to stay seated.

The Jordanian doctors were most kind and pleasant. The child with the cleft palate was to return in four months for further consideration while the lady with abdominal pain was kept for continuing workup. They wanted me to tour their facility, but curfew time in Mazar was close, and we needed to return promptly to our base camp. Later I was privileged to have more time and took several tours of their excellent tent-hospital facility.

I spent many similar days at Khorasan during my remaining weeks in February and later when I returned in April and May. During this time our NGO, Medical Teams International, helped by providing doctors, medications, and hospital costs when necessary for thousands of distressed patients. As I became more familiar with expectations and procedures I worked independently with a translator but continued to frequently discuss patients with our Afghan partners, as did they with us. It was a good arrangement.

Upon my return in the spring, this camp had under a thousand refugees remaining. Most of the tiny pup tents had been removed. The mud impregnated with fecal material remained. Various NGOs, nongovernment organizations, under the direction of UNOCHA, the United Nations Organization Coordinating Humanitarian Activities, had been working successfully to return refugees to their own villages. As incentives, they provided temporary shelters, food, and seed for planting, as well as some transportation. I was impressed that in general the refugees were grateful to be returning home.

Many of the patients we saw in Khorasan in the spring were not only from the camp but also from northern Mazar and some nearby villages. There was less pneumonia then but more gastroenteritis and chronic ailments. It was certainly needed care, but the decreased load enabled us to see patients in many other areas.

COUD-E-BARQ—A NEEDY, RUSSIAN-BUILT HOSPITAL

That morning for breakfast, in addition to the usual hot water for instant coffee, bread, butter and jam, we were treated with a small box of Kellogg's Cornflakes and a tiny bottle of canned milk. Hamayoun, our cook, had found this box in a small shop selling food items. The cornflake box was dated 05-26-98. Its content tasted wonderful!

I had awakened that morning looking forward to going to a tiny hospital about twenty kilometers west of Mazar City called Coud-e-Barq. It was in an area near an old, Russian-built fertilizer factory that was still operating. Many Russian-style apartment buildings and this tiny hospital had been constructed nearby. A few days before, we had visited with the hospital administrator, Dr. Noor, and some of his colleagues. They were eager to join with Medical Teams International in improving the hospital and helping to better serve the many without medical care both there and in surrounding villages. They would welcome any suggestions, and we assured them that we were also there to learn from them.

In touring the hospital it was obviously in major disrepair. It had not been painted for years. The dental room's equipment was totally broken down, and the dentist was now able to use it just for pulling teeth. There was only one ancient x-ray machine. Beds were old and rusty. The men's public bathroom was so soiled that one hated to enter it. Puddles of water with urine and some excrement covered much of the floor. In the surgical room was no monitoring equipment; old catheters were being resoaked in a large pan of yellow disinfectant, and the surgical table sagged on one side beneath its ancient stained pads. We were shown x-rays of some orthopedic procedures done recently and realized that, in spite of huge handicaps, Dr. Noor and his associates performed high-quality work. One of the Afghan doctors who worked with us assured us that if he were to need surgery, this would be where he would come.

We looked at several possible locations for our clinic and decided on two rooms at the east end of the main hospital building. These would need considerable cleaning up but did have one usable sink and a functional light bulb in each room. We assured them that our intent was not to take away from their paying patients, ones who could give a little amount, but to see only those without financial ability: the poorest of the poor

The highway to Coud-e-Barq was described by Amanolla, my interpreter for the day. He said it was "the best in all of Afghanistan." In spite of this reputation it was interrupted by much broken pavement and many deep chuckholes. The gateway into Coud-e-Barq was guarded by several soldiers, one of whom appeared to be an adolescent. After briefly inspecting our identification, they waved us through.

As we drove up to the little hospital at Coud-e-Barq we could see an Afghan lady standing on the steps just outside the clinic door waving a two-foot-long club. A sizable group of patients crowded near her feet. Many were talking insistently as she waved her club and shouted back. I learned soon that her name was Najma. She was not wearing the usual burqa, but had on a long-faded and tattered sweater that had probably been dark pink years before. An old blue dress peered from below that, and light-colored, baggy trousers covered her legs down to dark rubbers on her feet. A long cream-colored shawl was wrapped around her head and neck, leaving her face uncommonly uncovered. I thought this not only must help to make her shouting plainer but also gave more accuracy in wielding her club. (Later, after seeing crowd control attempts at many clinic sites, we realized she was doubtless among the best at this difficult job.)

I learned more about Najma during subsequent weeks through my interpreters and the Afghani doctors. You would have guessed her age to be much older than her thirty-five years. Her life had been difficult. This was her first paying job in four years. Her husband and brother had died in fighting near Kabul. Najma had three children at home, the oldest a thirteen-year-old boy. Food had often been scarce, provided by the kindness of friends. Hardship and grief lined her face, and only one tooth remained in her brief smile. (That tooth later became infected and was removed.) But she was determined to do a good job, and she did. Stories like Najma's are part of most people's lives in Afghanistan.

We saw many patients that day. My journal, written that evening, described several. One lady with advanced mitral heart valve disease had a rapid heart rate and mild peripheral edema (fluid in her legs). Her lungs were clear, but her heart was enlarged and the electrocardiogram had typical changes for this condition. We started her on medications to slow and strengthen her heart and remove excess fluid, and planned to see her again in a few days.

Many people had gastroesophageal reflux disease (acid backing up from the stomach into the esophagus). I thought this surprising since almost all of them were very thin. Generally, they were treated with acid blockers and antacids, instructed not to eat for a few hours before bedtime and to sleep with their upper body elevated.

I saw many with thyroid enlargement due to lack of iodine in their diet. Most I treated with iodized salt, available but not generally used in Afghanistan. One lady had a very large thyroid nodule. She was having trouble swallowing and demonstrated it by choking on a sip of tea. This case deserved a thyroid scan to look for cancer, and possibly a biopsy and esophageal scoping, as well as basic thyroid blood tests. However, such was not then available. (Later a gastroenterologist with MTI brought a scope and trained Dr. Rhamani to use it.)

My journal noted: "The weather is turning colder and damper, and we all have colds. Bill and Neil will be going home soon and possibly also Tom and Donna Armstrong. For a while that will leave only Tom, myself, and our Afghan doctor friends. At this time we had expanded our activities, and with a lesser staff I wonder how well we will survive." A line in my journal described some homesickness with this line, "And so, Jo, (my wife), it goes on, and I miss you dreadfully much."

I spent several days at the clinic in Coud-e-Barq, both during the winter stay and upon my return in the spring. I especially remember several patients. One lady had raging clinical hyperthyroidism (overactive thyroid) and was started on a beta-blocker and another thyroid hormone blocking agent. The latter was hard to find in Afghanistan. The two most commonly used ones in America were not available in Mazar, but after much searching a related medicine was found. Her proptosis (appearance of bulging eyes), shakiness, sweatiness, extreme nervousness, weakness, and rapid heartbeat were slightly better in one week and much better in two weeks. We tried to explain and arrange for long-term treatment, with the very real possibility that she might eventually need control through surgical removal of thyroid tissue.

Another young woman, in her midtwenties, was brought in by her father. She had had slowly progressive weakness in her legs and could no longer walk. They told me through the interpreter that a surgeon wanted to operate on her back after taking x-rays. She had no particular pain and no history of injury, and yet retained some sensation in her legs. They wished to have another opinion (just like us at home). She had findings of marked leg weakness, sustained clonus (repeated jerking) and hyperreflexia in tapping on her posterior ankle tendons(signs of upper motor neuron injury), and with normal reflexes in her arms the lesion was apparently in her spinal cord below the neck area. On inspecting her back carefully, no abnormal protuberance or gross malalignment was evident. I encouraged them to go ahead with the good surgeon who had x-rayed her. But many things went through my mind. Tumor? Multiple sclerosis? Injury that they didn't wish to mention? I so wished for an MRI scanner, certainly not available here and probably not in all of Afghanistan. She pulled her burqa about her face, and as her father knelt and bent in front of her, she reached her arms about his neck. He left the room carrying her on his back. Her legs dangled uselessly. There was no mistaking the sadness on their faces. What would become of her? *I felt devastated.*

One dad brought his little two-and-a-half-year-old boy. His concerns were several. The child had entered the world with a sizable lump at the base of his skull. It had enlarged as he grew and was now a bit bigger than a hen's egg. Since birth, the little one had crossed eyes and much leg weakness, even yet not being able to walk. Later, as I journeyed with them to see the neurosurgeon at the Jordanian hospital, the tremendous love reflected back and forth through the smiles of this father and son was profound. The lump might hold brain or spinal cord tissue as well as fluid. Surgery was arranged. I left Afghanistan before it was done and have not heard how this turned out.

"She is sad" was the complaint regarding one young woman. It was obvious in her face. Her husband had been killed in the fighting near Kabul a year before. Because of a lack of surety for good long-term follow-up, I seldom started antidepressants. But I did for this lady. She seemed a suicide risk. Two weeks later she was somewhat "better." On her return a man came in with her who was her dead husband's brother. She was now this brother's second wife. I hope they were able to keep her on the medicine for a few months before gradually tapering off.

A young mother and her tiny son were among these patients. As she sat down by the table near me my interpreter said, "They are starving. They come from a village far away." The tiny boy had stick-like legs and both had thin, old-appearing faces. I talked with them about several possibilities for getting food, but she felt none of these was possible. We had only a packet of biscuits but could give them each a supply of multivitamins to last several weeks. In leaving, she would need to keep the biscuits hidden under her burqa, or others would likely take them away from her.

So very often my limitations were apparent, and I had to say, *God, I put them in your hands*. Most Afghans would understand that.

BUZKASHI: SPORTING WITH DECAPITATED GOATS

Six weeks earlier I had heard in our US news of a Special Forces soldier competing in a game called "buzkashi" near Mazar-i-Sharif soon after the city was freed from Taliban control. I remember the article, which admired his courage while questioning the safety of the practice. It would have seemed unbelievable then to have been told that I'd soon be headed toward that same field of competition. Now, I was happy to be going only as a spectator, although accompanied by warnings of the possibility that some in the crowd hated us. We were to keep close together.

This contest generally consisted of two opposing groups of horsemen competing for the body of a decapitated goat. The goat was placed in a circle on one side of a large field. The objective was to reach down, lift the carcass up beside you, ride past a pole about one hundred meters away, and then return to the original circle. Others tried to battle their opponents for the goat. We were told that, historically, the body of an enemy was used.

During that winter I was privileged to watch this spectacle twice. Buzkashi had been banned during the Taliban rule.

Driving south from Mazar we passed the remnants of war: bombed-out buildings, destroyed tanks, and signs warning of land mines. Leaving the last of this ruin behind we could see several thousand people surrounding a large field with a backdrop of the Hindu Kush Mountains—huge red-rocked cliffs capped by snowy peaks glistening in winter sunlight. A grandstand holding perhaps a thousand spectators and roofed with blue sky also rose to the south of the field. From a distance we could see many horsemen alternately racing about, then bunching together, and then racing away again.

After stopping and disembarking we were told to keep a close eye on the horses and the movements of the crowd. Though the field was probably two hundred meters across, there was actually no boundary and the contestants might suddenly come riding through the surrounding spectators at breakneck speed. The entire throng was composed of men and boys. Hence Donna, Carol, and Mukhabat—the lady members of our medical team—were a novelty with their uncovered faces and drew about as much or more attention than the contest. Out of deference to the Afghan culture, they wore scarves over their heads. In watching the Afghan men, I sensed they generally rather enjoyed having these women there.

We were invited to come up into the stands and sit next to the mayor of Mazar-i-Sharif. It was a dense assemblage, but they kindly made way for us. The mayor briefly nodded but otherwise didn't acknowledge us. We learned the crowd was expected to contribute money toward the winning side of the contest. After adding ours to the pot, we sat down to watch. At the moment, a group of about forty fighting horsemen was bunched together a very few meters in front of us. Horses were pushing and rearing, and their riders were pulling and shoving, shouting and swinging heavily braided leather whips across each other. The contestants appeared thickly clothed and had covered heads. Many wore large fur Buzkashi hats. These were obviously needed, especially to lessen the effects of opponents' whips. Finally, one horseman leaning from his horse managed to pick the very tattered remnants of the goat from the ground and push away from the group, with several others in hot pursuit. They galloped furiously toward a distant pole, and the man carrying the goat was forced to drop it soon after rounding that marker as the battle for possession continued.

We saw that one horse had an empty saddle, and a rider lay stretched out on the ground nearby. Two comrades hurried over, dismounted, and seemed to be talking with him. A bit later he was helped on wobbly legs toward the spectators' stand.

Finally one rider appeared out of the entangled combatants and raced toward the starting point, dropping the remnants of the goat in that same circle. The shout from the crowd affirmed that this was a winning finish.

As we watched subsequent skirmishes, we learned more about buzkashi. The horses appeared well-kept, far different from the emaciated ones we saw pulling taxis and wagons. These and their riders must have been some of the cavalry of the Northern Alliance.

Leaving the stands, our group slowly found its way through the crowd on the east end of the field. By then we had our own large entourage of Afghan boys. There we also joined a sudden scrambling to avoid on-rushing horses and riders with "the goat." One of our group had lagged behind to get his shoes shined by a scraggly appearing lad. He was sitting on the ground when his vendor abruptly arose and ran, accompanied by the surrounding crowd. He looked up to see a galloping horse, with its rider clinging to the goat, and two others close behind. It was too late to run. He quickly prostrated himself while trying to protect his head with both hands. Others informed us that the three horses jumped right over him! (Don't you wonder if the shoe-shining job was ever finished?)

DOWNTOWN MAZAR-I-SHARIF

It is a place of contrasts. The Blue Mosque is a brilliant jewel on a large area of land in the middle of Mazar-i-Sharif. Its two blue domes glisten in the sunlight, and minarets reach toward heaven. Crowds of the Muslim faithful come and go—groups of women, faces covered, in flowing burqas, and robed men, turbaned or with small, close-fitting prayer hats. Flocks of hundreds of white doves alternately rise and settle among the trees and bushes that dot the lawns between paths surrounding the mosque. Five times a day loudspeakers broadcast forceful calls to prayer. It is obviously a place of much importance and is very well kept.

The streets reaching out from this center are lined with two- and three-story buildings containing small shops and businesses. Interestingly there are no large stores, but shops dealing with similar wares tend to be grouped together. Pharmacies were mostly down a street adjacent to the Public Health Hospital. Clothing stores seemed to be in another area and rug shops in yet another. Many vendors had carts along the street selling vegetables or fruit. Some sold used car parts or other wares from tarps or on bare ground near the street. One area was set aside for trading currency. Our Afghan friends did help greatly in exchanging dollars for Afghanis, the nation's currency, and tried to get us the best bargains.

Crowds were often dense, leaving little room to move. In maneuvering our way through these areas it wasn't difficult to recall that we'd been told of the $25,000 rewards posted around the city by Al Qaeda for each Westerner who was killed. Among ourselves we jokingly were happy that 80 percent of Afghans are illiterate.

Vendors of all sorts, as well as beggars with extensive deformities and amputations, were constantly asking for attention. Many men carried guns and grenade launchers. On the streets the flow of traffic seemed totally disorganized with burros, camels, sheep, and goats mixed in with the carts, trucks, ancient buses, and disintegrating little yellow taxis. Loads of brush for fuel and bags of grain for the hungry populace were common. At a few major intersections policemen who stood on small platforms waved and whistled without apparent effect. It was amazing how few accidents seemed to happen.

Crossing streets was at some personal peril, not only because of the chaotic traffic but because the median dividing the lanes also served as the public restroom. We had to watch where we stepped. It was common to see someone squatting there only concealed by long clothing.

Most shops were manned by one to three people and were small in space. "Manned" is certainly the correct word. Not a single lady shopkeeper was evident to my eye in all of Mazar-i-Sharif. On my first trip I did buy items to take back to family and friends such as hats and burqas. The rugs were especially outstanding, not only in quality but in price. I was told that a medium-size rug with gorgeous patterns and colors might have taken a single person working regularly as long as a year to weave. Such a rug, measuring eight or ten feet to a side, sold for about $300 during that winter and was a bit more expensive on my return six weeks later. Reimbursement to the weavers must have been even less than the dollar a day commonly paid by various nongovernment organizations for menial work.

We did see several "antique" rugs. Our understanding was broadened by observing some resourceful rug shops actually antiquing their rugs in the streets with the help of passing traffic: camels, taxis, and burros.

Among the shops were many other enterprising people, including eager shoeshine boys and people selling varied products, including a wheelbarrow full of live chickens with tied legs. Upon entering some small shops we took off our shoes. At one rug shop an eager lad quickly grabbed my shoes and began to shine them. There was no doubt of the need on both our parts, so I was glad to pay him well. Actually he accomplished a fine shine, and it lasted several weeks.

We frequented a wholesale pharmacy with our Afghan physician friends. It was small but had shelves crowded with a large variety of medications. Prices were much less than here at home. We had to rely on our friends' advice as to which products would less likely be adulterated with starch or sugar. In their opinion some were suspect.

During our time of work in the refugee camps and later in village clinics, we used huge amounts of medications. Gradually, we planned ahead better and avoided the bind of an inadequate supply. Major groups included antibiotics, medications for gastrointestinal problems, and those for cardiovascular ailments. Even though depression (sadness) was exceedingly common, we generally avoided antidepressant or tranquilizer type drugs.

On one pharmacy visit a lady entered behind us shouting and waving her arms. Her clothes were torn and filthy, and she had no covering over her deeply creased, angry-appearing face. The shopkeeper gave her a small amount of paper money and waved her away, explaining to us that she was a common troublemaker, and it was the only way to get rid of her.

In spite of some trepidation and uncertainties, our whole medical team was treated with courtesy and friendliness. Shopkeepers were generally eager to help. Other than some deeply angry stares, I never felt directly threatened and appreciated the mostly gracious ways of the Afghan people.

Often, in traveling those streets, I was amazed by the sights, sounds, and smells, and thought, "I would love for my wife and many people back home to see this astounding mixture of ancient and modern ways, of peace and distress." One scene remains most vivid: I saw two young boys in a vacant lot fighting vigorously; pushing, pulling, and striking with their fists. As a third lad ran toward them, I watched, wondering which side he would take. He pushed them apart.

One of the great privileges of travel with Medical Teams International has been getting to know outstanding people, many of whom have served repeatedly in disaster areas. With the risk and probability of omitting ones I should have mentioned, I will attempt recall of some others of these fellow travelers:

Dr. Tom, with whom I traveled to and from Afghanistan on my first trip. He was energetic, bright, kind, full of curiosity, and always exploring something. While waiting for the plane in Termez to fly back to Tashkent, we were in a crowded waiting room. The airfield was hidden. The steel door next to the airfield was closed but had a peephole near the locked latch. We heard a plane taxi up outside, and I said to myself, "Tom will want to take a look." In spite of the large number of people crowded against the door, Dr. Tom carefully edged his way through and bent to look and inspect the aircraft.

Dr. Neil is an emeritus professor from Oregon Health and Sciences University. Dr. Neil is a tall man, who always draws a crowd wherever he goes. He is thoughtful and kind, and a man of accomplishment and knowledge. What a wealth of medical experience he has had throughout the world. He is obviously very fond of his family and had their many pictures on the wall beside his sleeping area. Neil was full of good advice, such as, "Be sure to take plenty of pictures at the start of your tour. Later they will seem commonplace, and you may miss some you should have taken."

Dr. Bill, a fellow internist, is from Seattle. He is one of the kindest doctors I have known, a Harvard graduate with many years of medical experience. His compassion for the Afghan people was obvious. After he returned home, one of the Afghan workers commented, "You remind me of Dr. Bill." That was very high praise.

Near the end of my first assignment in Afghanistan, two replacements walked up the steps, Dr. Rick and Nurse Carol. Dr. Tom and I greeted them at the top. Immediately I had a deep perception that "these are good people." That first impression proved to be true. Rick is an anesthesiologist and left behind a young family, who he loved dearly. What great sacrifice. Dr. Rick subsequently did an outstanding job of assessing needs at the Coud-e-Barq hospital and starting the process for shipment of badly needed supplies and equipment.

Carol is an emergency room and critical-care nurse. She had been working in New York City when 9/11 occurred and was one of the first to ground zero. Now her compassion took her to the opposite side of the world to help other victims of Al Quaida. Carol has weathered severe personal grief, which helped her return to her roots. Out of that complex background, and as a Christ follower, flows huge richness of character. Carol served as in-country director of MTI for several months. Someday I hope someone writes the life story of this superb lady.

Fellow travelers, whether mentioned briefly or at more length, you have added hugely to my life. Thank you, each one.

SALAAM A LAKUM

On my first medical team to Afghanistan I served for four weeks. I felt I needed to return, so six weeks later I did so.

After being gone for six weeks I wondered what reception awaited me on my return to Mazar-i-Sharif. Crossing the desert made me very aware that in those few weeks spring had arrived in northern Afghanistan. It had even rained considerably, and in several lower areas dampness or even a little standing water was apparent. The desert showed a few splashes of green between the sand dunes. Wild poppies added beauty along the road and often displayed dabs of crimson above cracks in the pavement. I was happy to realize that on this stint I would be warmer.

Crossing the border between Uzbekistan and Afghanistan had been a lengthy process. Even though a United Nations agency had notified them that we would be coming, Jackie, a registered nurse with an enviable history of practicing medicine in the developing world, and Carrie, a capable nurse practitioner, were not listed on the Uzbek ledger. The delay added two hours to the lengthy process of permission to cross the Friendship Bridge. Brandon, who had been working to help restart the university in Mazar, came to pick us up in a Russian jeep-like vehicle. It always intrigued me how many problems this "new" vehicle exhibited. This time was no exception. As usual, its transmission complained audibly each time he attempted to shift gears, and it refused to restart at one checkpoint. Several Uzbek guards helped get it running again. Dusk was falling as the guard opened the locked gate of our compound in Mazar-i-Sharif. It pleased me to see the broad smile spread across his normally solemn face. A group of Afghan and American friends were gathered on the steps and small porch leading to our apartment. As we exited our van, we heard repeated greetings, "Salaam a Lakum, Dr. Ken." We greeted each other, placing our right hand over our hearts, shaking hands, hugs and kisses. I introduced Jackie and Carrie. They were also greeted warmly, but with the propriety shown between the sexes in this culture. We were deeply touched by the Afghans' profuse kindness.

That evening our Afghanistan coordinator, Carol, gave Jackie, Carrie, and me a thorough update on what was happening at our clinics. With the refugee camp at Khorasan mostly empty, that clinic was open only one day a week. The clinic at Koud-e-Barq was operating three days a week, and clinic work was expanding in the sixteen villages we had been assigned.

Of these, one village seemed resistant. Both the American and Afghan workers felt unfriendliness and a considerable sense of tension. Problems, such as the village leaders insisting that certain men be seen first and making the women crawl through a window in order to get to their exam area, only magnified our concerns. Consequently that clinic had been closed.

Brandon and I were assigned the smaller sleeping room near the dining area. Considering that the majority of our American workers were women, they bunked in the lower and larger bedroom. In addition to Carol the team already in the house included Deanna and Sandi, both very capable RNs with considerable overseas experience, and Rebecca, our secretary from Uzbekistan. They would soon be joined by Victoria, our superb disaster relief coordinator from Oregon.

AND THERE WERE SHEPHERDS KEEPING WATCH

On a Friday, a Muslim holy day, away from our care of patients in refugee camps and small villages, John Mohammed Nayab had driven several of us up into the Hindu Cush Mountains. Following a sandy river, high, red, rock cliffs bordered our narrow road. In some places bombs had left huge craters. We passed a twisted Taliban tank, mangled by air strikes occurring only a few weeks before. Rugged snowy peaks loomed to the south, attached to Pakistan eastward. At one place, where the steep canyon widened, a large flock of tan, black, and brown fat-tailed sheep grazed on a slope of green. Here John turned abruptly and forded the silted river with the Land Cruiser, crossed a tiny rise, and pulled up to a large hidden pool fed by a clear spring. Several Afghan men swam there in long clinging shirts and baggy trousers. Some of our group joined them. I waded. They seemed happy to see us and offered a plate of white mulberries—delicious!

While traveling back toward Mazar-i-Sharif, I interrupted our rollicking music and clapping to tell the driver, John Mohammed, that if the occasion presented itself, I hoped to get some pictures of a flock of sheep and their shepherds. That day we had seen several small herds of both goats and sheep, but none close to the highway. It surprised me when John almost immediately slowed, then left the paved road, driving down a steep embankment and out into the desert toward the northwest. My immediate thought was, *What about land mines?* Looking ahead, I was relieved to see the tracks of a single vehicle crossing the sand, but only dunes could be seen on the distant horizon. We followed as the tracks continued on, happily uninterrupted by any craters. A few minutes later we faintly could see the distant silhouette of a building rising out of the sand. It slowly took on the form of a small house with a domed roof and long adobe fence attached to the west side.

Two immense dogs came bounding toward our approaching van, barking and snarling, and three figures emerged from behind the hut. Before opening our car doors, it seemed wise to wait until their shepherd masters had grasped them by their collars and leashed them to posts. John Mohammed called greetings to these men and then to three others standing near a large band of sheep behind the corral area. Many embraces, much backslapping, and animated conversation followed. John Mohammed informed us that the shepherds and sheep were from his own village.

We Americans intermittently asked questions, and when I requested to take their picture, four of the shepherds quickly lined up in front of their band of sheep. Their dress code appeared to be "warm and comfortable." Four had fabric wrapped around their heads, some extending it to their neck and shoulders, and one had a small, close-fitting cap. Most had mustaches and beards, but the youngest made up for his smooth face with a fur Buzkashi hat. Several had an outer sweater or coat and under it the typical long shirt and baggy trousers. Footwear was entirely of sandals or slipper-like rubbers. No bright colors were evident, but rather the blues and grays and browns seemed tinted with the desert sands, adobe dust, and time.

The flock consisted of about two hundred sheep, both lambs and adults. They were not yet shorn, and, with the exception of blue, their coloration looked very similar to the clothing of their guardians. A few rams had long horns curled close to their heads. I could only imagine in this desert the sizable distances this flock must have to travel to find sufficient forage.

I asked how the large dogs, a bit smaller than Saint Bernards but of similar coloration, were used. The shepherds informed us that primarily they guarded the sheep from wolves and jackals. It is evident by both conformation and behavior that these dogs must be very effective.

Our arrival initiated a time of celebration, with our hosts extending to us most gracious hospitality. Invited inside the tiny hut, we sat in a circle, and the ever-present hot tea was poured. They cooked some mutton and served it in a pan, along with a few pieces of flat bread, both placed on a small, red, crocheted mat in the center of our circle. The meat was well seasoned and delicious. Several, including John Mohammed, took turns singing and dancing, accompanied by a flute-like instrument and small hand drum. The rest of us clapped in time to the music. What a pleasant time. This scene called forth many thoughts: *People of such different backgrounds, from exactly the opposite sides of the world, yet enjoying our time together. The setting might be little different from that experienced among shepherds in the time of Christ.*

While in this compound, I repeatedly felt the warm smile of one herdsman sitting across the small room from me. He had seen me at the clinic at Khorasan several days before for symptoms of esophageal reflux of stomach acid. It pleased me to hear he felt much improved.

A tiny black lamb was brought in for us to see and pet. It lay quietly beside the dish of mutton and seemed to enjoy the stroking. I guessed it to be an orphaned sheep—what we in America would call a "bummer lamb."

The kind hospitality enjoyed in this sheep camp was remarkable. Such has been my experience many times in Afghanistan, even being offered kindness by very poor people who could not really afford that excess. As we drove away we saw the little orphaned lamb snuggled up against one of the large guard dogs. We felt exquisitely gifted.

THE CIVILIAN HOSPITAL: (NOTES FROM MY JOURNAL)

"It is a privilege to frequently make patient rounds at the Civilian Hospital in Mazar-i-Sharif. I am impressed with the very intense efforts of those physicians to care for the Afghan people. We visited the military hospital once, but most of our ongoing associations took place at the civilian facility.

The hospital needs repairs badly. Walls have cracks, and peeling paint. A blanket tries to suffice for an exterior door in one place. Inside, old rusty beds support shabby bedding. Added niceties like chairs, bedside tables or lamps seem almost nonexistent. But I don't see trash. Cleaning people work vigorously, and it is obvious that health-care workers do well with what is available.

The Civilian Hospital has three main buildings and some smaller ones. One appears to be used primarily for orthopedics and surgery, another for gynecological problems and pediatrics, and the larger building for internal medicine, some offices, and separate rooms for men and women who need to be seen on an emergent basis. A lady internist told us that during the time of the Taliban she could only work in the section for women and children. To attempt to do otherwise would have resulted in sad repercussions. Most women were not allowed to work outside the home, so she actually felt fortunate. With many of the menfolks killed in the years of war, hardship on widowed mothers is often extreme.

As Jackie and I were walking up the front steps of the internal medicine building, we saw a young girl struggling to get a glass of water at a hand pump near the base of the stairs. She would pull the pump handle down and hurry to reach the spout with her cup on the opposite side; always too late to catch the water. As we stopped a bit to help, Jackie motioned for her to put the cup under the pump's spout while I worked the handle. The little girl collected her cup of water, gave us a sly smile, and hurried off.

It is most pleasant to greet Drs. Sidiqi and Yawsi and their Civilian Hospital entourage again. This is done with many "hellos" and "Salaam-a-Lacums." In addition to a few staff doctors there are four young physicians in their residency training. Together we proceed down a large and very dimly lit hall toward the several separate rooms for men and for women. Often family members collect there with the patients, some in the hallway and some hovering near the bed. It is routine for the resident in charge of a particular patient to present the patient's history and physical findings, much as we do during rounds in American hospitals. He stands near the head of the bed, and the others form a half circle around the foot of the bed. I try to listen closely as they relate history, physical findings, lab work, differential diagnosis, and plans. Lab work is unbelievably scanty, as I learned, because it is seldom available and, therefore, generally not done. After presenting the differential diagnosis and plans, Drs. Yawsi and Sidiqi, as well as others of the hospital staff, grill the young physicians with great intensity. Commonly a resident physician appears flustered, but disagreeing with his or her superior seems inappropriate. I do find myself feeling sorry for these young doctors. However, I also marvel at how well versed they are in Western medicine. Most speak English, at least to some extent. I am told that probably 80 percent of their schoolwork is done in English.

As we progress from bed to bed it falls my lot, as the eldest, to walk at the head of the group, and even to ask the first questions, if I so wish.

The Cardiac Care Unit for men is a room with about six patients. I did see one IV pole with attached IV fluids running, but otherwise there are no cardiac monitors, defibrillators, respirators, or even oxygen tanks. In listening to the stories of various men, and later women, it is good to see that the physicians have an old ECG machine and read the tapes accurately. Certainly lack of other equipment makes it impossible to practice ideal medicine, but they are doing very well under hard circumstances. Lab work commonly used in much of the world to verify myocardial injury is unavailable. Tests to help evaluate risks such as blood sugars and serum cholesterol are generally unused. Families are required to go to nearby pharmacies and purchase medications or IV fluids as prescribed by their doctor before the patient can receive them. If they have no money, the treatment is not done.

I especially remember one elderly man who had a large anterior infarction (heart injury) as shown by his ECG. In returning a week later I asked how that patient did. "Oh, he died of sudden death," his physician answered. Without a cardiac monitor they could only guess at the exact cause of his sudden death, so treatment is limited.

In another room is a frightened young man. His eyes are wide, his face sober, and his abdomen distended, full of ascites (fluid). He appears mildly jaundiced. The Afghan doctors feel it is most likely caused by cirrhosis; but with little lab work available, no scanning equipment, and no pathologist to inspect the easily obtainable ascitic fluid with a diagnostic needle tap, they are very limited as to possible causes and treatment. I am told that the most common source of cirrhosis and ascites in Afghanistan is due to chronic hepatitis from several types of infections. I wonder.

Under rumpled covers in an old rusty bed lies a very ill lady. Her respirations are rapid. She appears pale and extremely thin. The resident physician presents her as being just over forty years of age, though she looks much older. She has been coughing thick green and bloody sputum for two years. Her chest x-ray, held up to the light of a nearby window, shows bilateral lung infiltrates. Gently pulling back the covers I see much peripheral swelling (edema) and emaciated musculature. She moves weakly. Recently a dipstick placed in her urine showed signs of diseased kidneys. Blood pressure is low, only about 80/30. We discussed possibilities and concur that most likely all of this represents tuberculosis, both pulmonary and renal. I am sad that the hospital has no ability to culture or stain body fluids. The reality is that she has been brought to this facility far too late. (A day later she died.)

In the spring, on my second visit to Afghanistan, we Americans were not nearly the curiosity we'd been initially during that winter. Various NGOs had paid visits to the Civilian Hospital. MTI has been able to teach some procedures, such as ultrasonography and upper gastrointestinal endoscopy, and to furnish some medical textbooks, many needed stethoscopes, and blood pressure cuffs. In talking with Dr. Yawsi and others at the Civilian Hospital, there is frustration, as several promised items from various NGOs for diagnosis and treatment are very slow in materializing. We too feel the frustration. Initially we talked in terms of two or three months for orders to arrive. Much later we understand that it takes half a year for many things to make the trip, clear customs, and finally arrive for distribution. I wonder at so many delays.

Nevertheless, as I ponder I thank you, my Afghan physician friends, for all you have taught and are yet teaching me. Thank you also that you care so very much for your patients.

THE TALIBAN—RECENT STORIES

During my time in Afghanistan I heard the stories of many people under the Taliban rule. These stories need to be remembered. Everyone in Afghanistan has a story, generally of terrible tragedy.

Monsoor had gone to the Blue Mosque and was leaving when wild shooting began.

The Taliban had been given permission by their leader to shoot anyone they wished for three days. As he ran, a woman near him was shot dead. He jumped into a nearby ditch and lay quietly until dark, then carefully made his way home. His family was so glad to see him. He believes about five thousand people were randomly shot in those three days.

Along with many other men, Monsoor's father had been forcefully crowded into a sizable truck shipping container. This one was made of heavy plastic, and the men were able to make a hole in the side to get some cooling and fresh air. Monsoor searched many containers that night looking for his dad. He sadly relates generally getting no response from within the metal-walled containers; the occupants had died of suffocation. He was feeling very discouraged when he reached the last container. Calling out, several voices answered, including the voice of his dad. What a relief! He wept as he hurried home to return soon with food and water. His father and the others survived. The family fled to Pakistan.

Nadia was not eager to talk about it. Her father had been shot right in front of her and her mother. Now her elderly mother had suffered a heart attack, and Nadia was staying by her side at the Civilian Hospital.

Mertaza was about ten years of age, and he recalled fierce fighting, and especially the horror of seeing body parts hanging in a tree.

Abdullah was trying to study medicine. Between long hours at the hospital and reading textbooks, he was exhausted. Without regard for his need to sleep, the Taliban insisted that he get up at five each morning to pray. He related that generally sports such as kite flying and soccer were forbidden. Most music was prohibited, and people could dance only when they were able to post a guard to watch for approaching Taliban.

Ajmal spent nearly a year in jail because he had shaved his beard too short. The prisoners were crowded together, had little food, and were frequently beaten. He feels fortunate to have survived.

Tamim is married to one of the sisters of a Northern Alliance officer. This made him a special outcast. He was jailed and beaten often. Tamim is convinced he could not have lived had he not been a big man.

One day while traveling to a village over adobe roads made greasy-slick by recent rain, our nineteen-year-old translator began telling of his recent experiences with the Taliban. He commonly was a spectator at the trials, sentencing, and execution of sentences of many lawbreakers. He recalls watching as the Taliban cut off the arms of thieves. One man, who had caused a death, had his throat slashed. Another was hanged, and many others were executed by shooting. Our translator recalled one occasion when the accuser decided that the offender should not be killed, and withdrew his complaint. The crowd of spectators cheered. One physician said, "Even if two members of my family have been killed by American bombs, it was worth it to be free of the Taliban."

Even though it was extremely rare to see a woman without a burqa and facial covering in public, obviously there seemed to be a mixture of attitudes between men and women. These perspectives go far back before the Taliban era. One woman we knew well was asked, "When are you going to quit wearing your burqa?" She replied, "When the men lay down their guns." Another woman, when asked about taking her picture while her face was uncovered in the clinic, quickly covered her face and replied, "If my husband should see my picture with face uncovered, he would kill me." I asked a woman carrying a beautiful young child near the Civilian Hospital if I could take the child's picture. Her nearby husband quickly stepped over, grabbed the child for the picture, and pushed his wife behind him. He did all this in spite of the fact that she was well-covered in the usual fashion.

We enjoyed eating in several Afghan homes. Always, the women stayed hidden and cooked in the kitchen area. The women with Medical Teams International ate with the men but were also privileged to go to the kitchen areas and visit with the Afghan women. Not so for us men. We saw a sense of celebration among most of the Afghans. Returning from trips to the villages we often saw beautiful kites flying over the houses. Occasionally we saw boys playing a game of soccer or volleyball. At one place kids played excitedly on a homemade merry-go-round. People were free to buy and play music, both instrumental and with singing. Sometimes during the drive back from a distant village, the music in the Land Cruiser would really rock. I felt a bit of concern when the driver took both hands off the steering wheel to join in the clapping. Thankfully that happened rarely.

CLINICS IN AFGHAN VILLAGES

While working to spread medical help to some sixteen villages near Coud-e-Barq, our reception varied enormously. These little towns of one thousand or two thousand people had almost no medical care. Most appeared very happy to see us come. Some seemed much less so. The leaders in one village gave their okay grudgingly.

Another village was remote, but what an interesting and needy place. We took the road again to Coud-e-Barq, maneuvering through broken pavement and huge potholes, then onto a back road, made greasy slick with rain. Along the way to the village we saw some amazing sights. A camel, neck stretched out, rested its head on a patient burro. Many flocks of fat-tailed sheep and multicolored goats roamed the fields. A newborn camel stood with trembling legs next to its mother. We saw people following the road edges toward their fields carrying large-bladed hoes over their shoulders. Some burros were being ridden, and others were pulling small carts. We met a large truck loaded with Afghan soldiers holding rifles and grenade launchers. Deep inside I realized a bit of fear at this vivid reminder of the waiting dry tinder of factional animosities. Small villages had clusters of adobe houses with their metal roofs peeking over purposefully high clay walls. At a few small intersections our driver stopped and asked local men, "Which road will take me to Al Tajik?"

Dipping down toward a very narrow, muddy bridge, I swallowed and clenched my teeth, wondering if its width would carry our Land

Cruiser. The bridge had no side rails, and it crossed a large, dirty, rapidly flowing irrigation canal. While holding my breath, I felt glad that John Mohammed Nayab was our driver. About a hundred meters farther up a small slope was a waiting crowd of both adults and children clustered tightly in front of a small, vacant building.

John told us that many years before it had been a hospital, but it had closed when the Taliban ruled.

An elderly man stepped out from the edge of the crowd. He had a slender, weather-beaten face above a full gray beard. A white turban capped his head while a dark blue vest and belt contrasted with a long white robe. He was the village chief and mullah. John introduced us, and we each in turn bowed slightly, placed our right hand over our heart, said our Afghan greeting (Salaam a Lakum), and shook hands. He seemed sincerely glad to see us. We followed him into a room in the front of the old hospital with our bags and trunks of medicines and equipment. The old chief related that some other NGOs had been reluctant to come and give help because UNICEF had labeled this town as an "Al Quaida village." He quickly told us, "This is not true. Our girls' school has restarted, and we have two grades for both boys and girls. But we have no paper or pencils or books."

Sick and curious villagers crowded close. Kids packed together to peer through the windows. We taped plastic bags over those few windows and put up small screens to give some privacy. Four young men were appointed by the mullah to guard the doorway. One served as the gate, with back against one side of the doorway and braced foot on the other. He held a rifle. The other three tried to keep the outside crowd controlled. Lots of noise didn't help my old ears.

The first few patients had sizable problems, including several with heart problems. The findings of one patient with severe facial sores appeared consistent with cutaneous leishmaniasis (a protozoan that may burrow under the skin—extremely rare in the United States). Patients tended to be less critically ill as the day progressed. They managed to wiggle their way past the guards, and by the end of the day they crowded around us, fueled by curiosity. The four guards had seemingly given up on crowd control.

Midway through the morning I slipped out to the nearby latrine. Suspended on stilts, it had a round hole in the floor with filthy edges above a deep ditch. It drained down the slope toward the brown water of the racing irrigation ditch. I had been told that in some villages it had become common to give tiny babies unboiled water from a canal as a test of their strength to survive.

At noon we were invited by the elderly village chief, the mullah, to his home to eat. We drove up a narrow, muddy road to a heavily gated yard. A tethered cow and donkey greeted us inside that gate. Escorting us into the house, a servant then seated us in a circle on a beautiful red, black, white, and brown rug with exquisite patterns. (I wondered how many months or even years it had taken a weaver to make such a rug.) They seated me to the right of the mullah. Several other men from his village joined us. Our group included two Afghan doctors; John Mohammed, our driver; Amanolla, a tall Afghan translator; and Jackie, a superb and very experienced American nurse. She covered her head with a scarf, and they graciously accepted her in this otherwise male group.

The waiting meal consisted of boiled potatoes, rice, yogurt, bits of mutton in the rice, and the ever present chai (tea) poured from a very ornate pitcher. Our meal was preceded by ritual hand washing. An attendant slowly rounded the group, pouring lukewarm water on each pair of hands with a large bowl underneath. We were each then given a drying towel.

John Mohammad explained to the mullah that our group commonly spoke a prayer before meals. The mullah replied that they liked to give a prayer at the end of their meals and demonstrated the motion that followed: with both hands lying on his lap, palms upward, he raised them to his head, turned the palms downward, and brought them back to his lap. Both expressions to God were used at that meal, adding to the sense of unity.

I was reminded again of Afghan realities as we finished our meal. We each shared about our families. I thought it a good time to show the mullah a picture of my wife, children, and grandchildren.

I retrieved the photo from my wallet and handed it to him. As he started to look at it he seemed almost startled and very abruptly handed it back. I belatedly remembered that in their Muslim culture it was not appropriate for a man to look at the uncovered hair and face of a woman not of their own family. I felt sad to have made him uncomfortable.

As we finished eating, the chief asked if Jackie would see his wife, who "had a fall." After seeing the wife in a different part of the house, Jackie asked if she could return with me later, after clinic, and together see the wife. The mullah agreed, and we did return that evening.

She appeared to have two treatable problems: PSVT, (episodes of very rapid heartbeat) and significant reflux of stomach acids into her esophagus. We had medicines and also advice regarding eating and positioning after meals. They were grateful.

We felt it was a good day at this small clinic.

CHOSEN

Words like dependability, endurance, and patience best describe the burros of Afghanistan. Only once did I see one acting up—a small colt cavorting and galloping along the roadway leading out of Mazar-i-Sharif. Its long neck rope flew behind, and a young lad scurried after. *I think that little donkey was laughing.*

Countless scenes cross my mind: burros carrying huge loads of brush and weeds out of the Hindu Kush Mountains and desert areas, to be used for fuel through the cold winter; some burros pulling carts carried the driver and a variety of produce; riders with feet almost dragging, and their little animal friends clip-clopping along beneath them without apparent complaint.

One day, coming over a rise on our way back from a village clinic, there abruptly appeared a group of nearly thirty riders, all on donkeys. The riders were armed with shovels and hoes, obviously on their way from work in the fields. In spite of the precipitous encounter with our van, the little animals quickly stepped aside, and we continued on.

On several occasions various ones in our group, both American and Afghan, asked if they could ride one of the little critters. Their owners were always happy to oblige, and in fact rather seemed to have fun watching us Westerners show our "burro-manship" (or lack thereof). Our mounts without exception seemed patient.

Commonly we would see a burro standing quietly with its load above or a cart behind, tethered only by a feedbag pulled up over its muzzle. One I especially recall was standing in the cold wind in front of the office compound of the United Nations Organization for Coordinating Humanitarian Activities. As we left an hour or more later, it was still there and seemed not to have moved a bit.

(This was the very spot where recently, in 2011, a bomb exploded, killing many of the UN staff.)

Much taller camels, on the other hand, are often smelly and cantankerous. One day we were impressed to see a burro standing at the edge of a field with a nearby camel resting its long neck across that donkey's back.

Although most of the tiny burro colts appeared clean and cuddly, an occasional one looked unkempt and dirty. I especially recall a dark little burro standing alone on the median near the Civilian Hospital. Its winter coat was bedraggled and soiled. Hair stood in clumps pointing in all directions. That little donkey's head hung down, appearing bent by the weight of sadness. I thought, *Perhaps this would be the one our Leader would choose. He would feed it, wash off the dirt, curry out the tangled hair, scratch around its ears, and hug its neck. Then together they would ride into Jerusalem.*

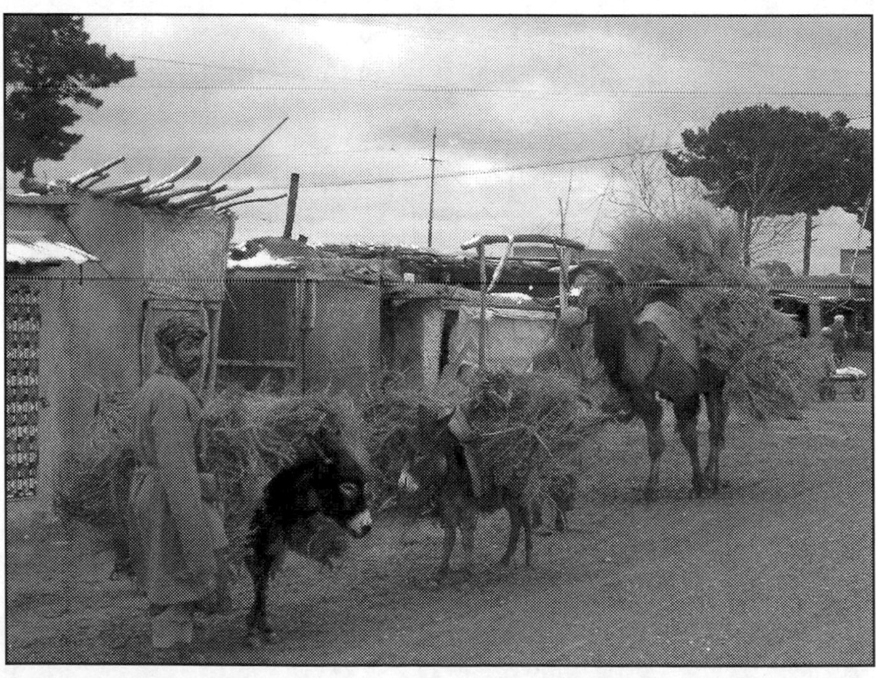

LETTERS TO AND FROM PRESIDENT BUSH

Right after 9/11, and in the next few years, I voiced some of my concerns by mail to President Bush and am pleased that he responded several times. I thanked him in return. Some of my letters and his replies are on the following pages.

Kenneth K. Magee, M.D.
5233 Uhrmann Rd.
Klamath Falls, OR 97601
Sept. 20, 2001

Hon. George W. Bush
1600 Pennsylvania Ave. N.W.
Washington, DC, 20500

Dear Mr. Bush:

As part of the desire for justice and to end terrorism I would urge you and our country to WAGE PEACE. I know this must be a concern of yours also. I don't want the circle of violence to be perpetuated as it has through much of history. To me it would seem an equal crime to retaliate by killing the innocents of the world. I appreciate your restraint.

I know you are a Christ-God follower and I know this is what He teaches. My prayers are with you in the difficult path you have to walk.

Sincerely,
Kenneth K. Magee

Kenneth K. Magee, M.D.
5233 Uhrmann Rd.
Klamath Falls, OR 97601
November 26, 2002

Honorable George W. Bush, President
1600 Pennsylvania Ave., NW
Washington D.C. 20500

Dear President Bush:

It is my wish to encourage my government to strive vigorously to wage peace in Afghanistan. I wish to add my voice to those asking for much more effort toward reconstruction in that country.

It was my privilege to serve with Northwest Medical Teams in the winter and again in the spring of this year in and around Mazar-i-Sharif. I was pleased with the amount of humanitarian aid coming into the country at that time. As important as or even more so than the many lives saved by our and others' effort was the hope and mutual appreciation created with the Afghan people.

Most people in Northern Afghanistan at that time were glad Americans were there. Not only did I become very attached to hurting peoples, but I do not want them to lose that hope in us. The vast majority of Afghans want peace and progress away from their suffering.

Certainly there are large obstacles such as the factional fighting in Afghanistan. May both our public plan and measureable action be to aggressively wage peace by forwarding the reconstruction of this country.

Only then will our motives be tolerable to the many nations of this world.

President Bush, I do pray for you and also for President Karzai much. Thank you for hearing my plea.

Sincerely, Kenneth K. Magee, M.D.

THE WHITE HOUSE
WASHINGTON

February 19, 2003

Kenneth K. Magee, M.D.
5233 Uhrmann Road
Klamath Falls, Oregon 97601-9312

Dear Dr. Magee:

Thank you for your letter about Afghanistan. I appreciate hearing your concerns and welcome youı suggestions.

As our Nation fights terrorism around the world, we remain fully committed to building a future of progress and stability for the Afghan people, and to ensuring the safety of those providing aid in thє region. The United States has helped Afghanistan avert mass starvation, reopen schools for both boys and girls, and establish the most broadly representative and accountable government in that country's history. We are helping the men and women of Afghanistan claim their democratic future, establish public order and safety, and we are working closely with the Afghan government tı overcome the forces of terror.

America will continue to work with the Afghan people to assemble institutions that will help their country develop peacefully, and in their image, not America's. Starting with the Tokyo Conferencє in January 2002, the United States and 60 other countries have pledged to provide $4.5 billion over five years to aid in long-term economic reconstruction, and the United States has provided nearly $850 million for humanitarian assistance, reconstruction, and recovery projects in Afghanistan. Wє are helping to reestablish security institutions including the Afghan National Army, and to restore infrastructure, clear mine fields, improve health care, and integrate women into the workforce. Our Nation and our partners are rebuilding roads, bridges, waterways, and buildings, and in September 2002, the United States, Japan, and Saudi Arabia committed $180 million to reconstruct the highway connecting Kabul, Kandahar, and Herat.

Since October 2001, more than 2 million Afghan refugees have returned to their homeland, and more than 3 million children have returned to school in Afghanistan. Afghan girls now comprise 30 percent of the total student population. Newspapers, radio, and television have been reborn, and individual, political, and religious freedoms are being reestablished. Women doctors are returning to work, and male doctors are once again allowed to treat women. Thanks to this progress, Afghanistan has entered a new era of hope, and the United States will continue to help its citizens recover from many years of tyranny and oppression.

Thank you again for writing. Best wishes.

Sincerely,

George W. Bush

March 3, 2003Kenneth K. Magee
5233 Uhrmann Rd.
Klamath Falls,OR 97601

President George Bush
The White House
Washington, D.C. 20502

Dear President Bush:

I very much appreciated your recent response to my letter of concern for ongoing help for Afghanistan.

Having spent considerable time in various needy parts of the world including Afghanistan, I realize how dependant on American help much of the world is. I have also seen the appreciation of these peoples for America. It is my prayerful hope that some way this may remain our primary focus. I have grave concern for the effects of the planned war in this part of the world on my country, America, and our ability to continue or increase aid.

President Bush, my prayers are much for you and your advisors. How difficult is your role.

Sincerely,
Kenneth K. Magee, M.D.

THE WHITE HOUSE
WASHINGTON

July 22, 2003

Kenneth K. Magee, M.D.
5233 Uhrmann Road
Klamath Falls, Oregon 97601-9312

Dear Dr. Magee:

Thank you for your kind words of support and for remembering me in your prayers.

At this time of great consequence for our Nation, I am honored to lead our country. We pray for the safety of the men and women who serve around the world to defend our freedom. We also pray for God's peace in the affairs of men. And we thank God for our Nation's many blessings. I appreciate knowing that I can count on your support as my Administration continues to work on issues that are important to Americans.

Laura joins me in sending our best wishes.

Sincerely,

George W. Bush

KENNETH K. MAGEE, M.D.
Physician
5233 Uhrmann Rd.
Klamath Falls, OR 97602
December 2, 2003

Honorable George W. Bush, President
1600 Pennsylvania Ave., NW
Washington, DC 20500

Dear President Bush:

It is my wish to encourage you and my government to continue to strive vigorously to wage peace in the Middle East.

Recently I spent several weeks with Northwest Medical Teams International teaching aspects of emergency medicine in northern Iraq. As you know, these are people who have suffered terribly at the hands of Saddam's regime. I found much jubilation that America is there and much hope for the future. I was encouraged not only by their hopeful attitudes but also by the reality of many individuals and groups from other countries that are trying to help. Some have been there for years.

One of these is Peter, a European who works with an organization teaching literacy to women and helping to upgrade their status. He feels strongly called by God to do this. Peter states, "I am basically a pacifist who feels the international community dropped the ball in dealing with the atrocities of Saddam's regime. I hated to see war, but now that you are here, please don't abandon us." These dear people inspire me to speak the same.

Thank you also for your help for Afghanistan. I appreciate that and am personally finding ongoing ways to encourage some in my profession in that country.

My prayers will remain with you that you may have God's wisdom. Thank you for hearing my pleas.

Sincerely,
Kenneth K. Magee, M.D.

THE WHITE HOUSE
WASHINGTON

January 14, 2004

Kenneth K. Magee, M.D.
5233 Uhrmann Road
Klamath Falls, Oregon 97601-9312

Dear Dr. Magee:

Thank you for your kind words of support and for remembering me in your prayers.

Our Nation has confronted great challenges, and we are meeting the tests of our time with courage, clarity, and resolve. During this time in history, I ask all Americans to pray for the safety of our brave men and women in uniform and for God's peace in the affairs of men.

I am grateful for your support as my Administration continues to work on issues important to the American people. May God bless you, and may God continue to bless our Nation.

Sincerely,

George W. Bush

GENE—MY HERO

June 28, 1992: A flock of white pelicans caught my eye. Their beautiful black-tipped wings reflected light while they circled gracefully above the south shore of upper Klamath Lake. They seemed to be staying close above the spot toward which I headed—the home of Dr. Gene and Millie Howard. My friend, Gene, suffered with a very aggressive form of cancer.

I connected with Dr. Howard in 1967, and we soon joined forces in Klamath Falls. I came. He left the very next day on vacation for a month. He had told me, "If another internal medicine doctor doesn't come to Klamath Falls soon, I'll be leaving permanently." I soon found out why.

In those days there were few medical subspecialties in Klamath Falls, and after the month of Gene's absence, I had utmost respect for his previous ten years of endurance. He and I took care of most complicated aspects of heart, lung, gastrointestinal, endocrine, and other nonsurgical adult diseases. We both took our turns with other doctors in the emergency room, and Gene or I was on call both day and night. Initially there was no Intensive Care Unit. Workweeks often exceeded eighty hours. We were expected to take on any new complex patients regardless of exhaustion. During his month of absence, I felt paranoia creeping in, and I met Gene's return with celebration. He became my hero.

During that first month he had returned to northern India, the land where he was born in 1924. Both he and his wife, Millie, had grown up there as children of missionary parents. Seeing the imposing mountains, the beautiful hills, and rushing rivers, and enjoying the people he and Millie had known for years renewed his energy.

He related many stories, such as that of Sahdu Sundar Singh, an Indian holy man who also became a Christ follower. Sahdu lived peacefully with wild animals, even with tigers. Sadhu had visited Millie's family just before disappearing forever into the rugged mountains north of India's border.

Gene and Millie had met while they were attending boarding school in northern India at Woodstock. It was at sixty-five hundred feet in the foothills of the Himalaya Mountains. He spent several years as a navy medic during World War II. They later married after he was enrolled in Baylor University School of Medicine. He graduated in 1951, completed a three-year residency program in internal medicine at Kansas City General Hospital, and came to Klamath Falls in 1957. They raised three most fortunate children.

In 1967, when I completed my residency in New Mexico, my wife and I had prayerfully searched for where we should go. There were many opportunities. It boiled down to either a leprosarium in Burundi, Africa, or our final choice of Klamath Falls, Oregon. Very soon after our decision we found out from a dear cousin in Burundi that we'd avoided a catastrophe. Thousands died in fighting between Hutus and Tutsi tribes. Many of their friends were killed, and our cousin and his family endured six months of house arrest.

Upon our arrival in Klamath Falls, Gene and Millie welcomed us warmly. At that time they and their children lived in a beautiful stone-faced house not far from the hospital. We often visited.

While making rounds at the hospital, Gene and I commonly met late in the evenings. It seemed convenient to pull up a couple of chairs at the ward nurses' station. The nurses were most accepting of our intrusions. Gene and I laughed and cried together. Not only did we discuss our patients and families but also what we were learning on our inner journeys. We did not always agree, but it became very therapeutic. It relieved the weight of "compassion fatigue." To Gene, his patients were all very important, whether the town mayor or a homeless person. Money was not his primary concern. He taught me much.

We discussed an elderly lady with cancer who hovered on the edge of death—she had been hospitalized for nearly a month. Two sons would come by daily and tell her, "Mom, keep fighting. You can make it! Don't give up." Finally Gene had gotten her sons together and carefully explained the situation. The sons better understood and accepted the finality of her situation. They went to their mother, kissed and hugged her, and said, "Mom, it's okay to let go now. We love you much." A few hours later she slipped away peacefully.

Once I told of falling asleep while palpating the abdomen of a lady that afternoon. I was glad that the sleep was brief and that I hadn't collapsed beside her exam table. I hoped she thought in my pause that I was just being extra careful. Gene and I laughed together.

Gene was an extraordinary lover of mountains. He climbed all the peaks in the Cascade Mountains. Nearby he climbed fourteen-thousand-foot Mount Shasta in northern California sixty-six times, and also returned to the Himalaya Mountains of Asia to climb peaks close to Mount Everest. He and Millie together climbed to the 17,600-foot base camp on Everest. In yet another expedition, led by the renowned Lute Jerstad, he and Lute made the first successful ascent of 20,600-foot M-6. He loved life.

I still treasure the hand-whirled prayer wheel he brought back to me. We worked together as the lone internists for several years prior to the most welcome addition of other good internists and specialists. Gene served in many medical associations, was the medical director of a large nursing home, and was director of the infirmary at Oregon Institute of Technology.

Gene developed a very aggressive form of prostate cancer in 1991. In his last six months, I was impressed by his deep sense of inner peace. It was June 28, 1992, when I saw the circling pelicans above Gene and Millie's lakeshore home. He had just "crossed over." Later, as I turned to leave, I glanced out of the large picture window overlooking the nearby lake. The pelicans skimmed just above the water's surface, doing a V-formation flyby.

IRAQI WARS

Saddam Hussein was part of the Ba'ath Party in Iraq, which rose to power by way of a coup in 1968. Saddam held the post of chief of the party's intelligence services initially. He became the primary leader of Iraq in 1979. The Ba'ath Party, largely secular in nature, faced not only economic stagnation but large protests from the Shia community in Iraq. Escalating conflict over the border with Iran brought about their invasion of Iran and war from 1980 until a cease-fire in 1988. In 1987 Saddam's cousin, Ali Hassan al-Majid, nicknamed "Chemical Ali," led poison gas attacks on the Kurds of northern Iraq, who had largely sided with Iran. Thousands died during the use of this "weapon of mass destruction."

The fragile Iraqi economy was further weakened by lower oil prices, leading to Hussein's threat to invade Kuwait if they did not decrease their oil production. Kuwait did not, and Iraq invaded Kuwait, leading to worldwide reaction and the Gulf War in the 1990s. There was ongoing concern about Iraq preparing weapons of mass destruction. This lead to the second massive invasion of Iraq by the United States, the United Kingdom, Australia, and Poland on March 19, 2003.

Turmoil remained in much of Iraq, but the predominantly Kurdish-controlled north settled more quickly. Medical care had been at a standstill for years. Broken and impoverished families were usual. It was into this suffering that Medical Teams International sent help.

IS GOD IN IRAQ?

It seems everyone in Iraq has his or her own story of tragedy. Asad was hoeing weeds in his recently planted hillside garden when two Iraqi warplanes came over a distant ridge. As he hurried his family into a nearby basement shelter having thick cement walls and large overhead beams, he heard a distant series of thuds. These sounded unlike those of a previous bombing. A bit later, while huddling in their hillside shelter, the wind brought a smell similar to old garbage and then another like apples.

Asad related, "The family's eyes began to water and our skin burned. The children felt short of breath and began crying. We knew that there were chemicals in the air and that we must leave."

With feelings of dread, Asad hurried his family out of the basement and up the nearby hillside. It was difficult to carry little Sabri. Below they could see a fog-like cloud blowing across their village. Some of the people, like themselves, were struggling to get away from their homes. Many lay on the ground. Their own cow was on its side nearby, not moving.

That day in April of 1987 marked the beginnings of the use of poison gas by Saddam Hussein's forces against the Iraqi Kurds. Five villages in Balisan Valley were hit. Over two hundred of Asad's neighbors died.

He adds the following story:

> Three days later some smoke from the poison gas remained in the valley. It was quiet except for a

> few sad voices and the bleating of a goat blinded by mustard gas trying to find its young. Abruptly, two of Saddam's Gazelle helicopters appeared and flew low over the valley. They then fired their heavy machine guns toward a nearby mountain pass. I went to see what had happened and found five of our villagers who had lived through the gas attacks now dead. One was a mother whose small baby had survived and was yet sucking milk from her breast. I will never forget that picture. It was horrible!

It is estimated that in all probably two hundred villages in northern Iraq experienced gas attacks, killing nearly two hundred thousand Kurds.

Halabja, not far from the Iranian border, was one of those hardest hit. It survives not far from the front lines of the Iran-Iraq war, and its eighty thousand inhabitants supported the Peshmerga, the Kurdish resistance fighters whose name means "those who face death." Some five thousand Kurds died during the gas attacks on Halabja. A memorable symbol of the suffering is a statue made from a picture showing a Kurdish man lying on the ground shielding the body of an infant, both dead from poison gas.

While taking a bag of dirty clothes to be washed down uneven stairs to the front desk of our hotel in Irbil, I stepped off the last riser and saw a middle-aged lady who spoke to the clerk with accented English. She smiled, and we talked. She was German, a forensic archaeologist. She had come here to help Iraqis open mass graves and to teach them how to identify remains. Did I hear correctly—there are nearly six thousand such barrows in Iraq?

I heard many stories of atrocities. One tells of the ailing victims of a gas attack fleeing to another town only to be corralled and buried alive.

Dr. Barzani, a stately middle-aged man who dresses in a neat dark suit, is director of the medical school hospital in Irbil. Sitting across from me as our team enjoyed an evening meal, he told of the tragedy that enveloped his family. Iraqi troops carried orders from Saddam Hussein to kill every Kurdish male in northern Iraq between the ages of eighteen and fifty-five. Nearly eight thousand men and boys had been taken from their hometowns and were never heard from again. Fortunately, he had been gone at the time, but several uncles vanished. Rights groups state that more than one hundred thousand men and boys disappeared during that campaign alone.

Nasreen is a widow who had five sons. She was told she could keep two, and the other three were taken and became part of the genocide.

Driving through northern Iraq, I was impressed by the numerous huge gray prisons. All are built exactly alike: square with long, straight walls, two stories high with circular bulwarks at each corner. Some stood alone, but west of Kirkuk, near the border of Kurdish territory, there were five of these massive structures. What great suffering they undoubtedly represent.

We passed many villages that were mostly heaps of rubble. Nearly four thousand in northern Iraq had been dynamited and bulldozed—about 80 percent of the total villages. Many people had become refugees to more northern areas, and one and a half million Kurds had fled Iraq.

It was in this setting with this history that our medical team began its work. Is it no wonder we questioned, "Is God in Iraq?"

A CHILD'S PERSPECTIVE

A few weeks have gone by since my return from Iraq with Medical Teams International. I have pondered much about what needs to be said. And so I speak, not as an expert but with deep impressions from my perspective, influenced by what I saw, heard, felt, and even smelled and tasted. The writings of Richard Rohr in *Everything Belongs*, the writer Matthew, the "IRS agent" who describes "blessings," and the following excerpt especially influence my understandings:

"How we image God matters." This is true of Iraq. Esther Armstrong, in *Journey into Freedom*, October, 2003, illustrates this reality by telling the following lovely story:

> Some time ago I spent a day with a very wise little boy. Josh has a vivid imagination. I knew we were going to spend quite a few hours together, so I asked my young friend with unruly curly hair, and wearing green Oshkosh B'Gosh bib overalls, what he would like to do. Without hesitation, he declared, "Find God."
>
> With a trace of adult cynicism I inquired, "Where would we find God?"
>
> "In the park," he answered matter-of-factly.
>
> I agreed to accompany him, but I admit I undertook our day's agenda with a mixture of curiosity and skepticism. Since I suspected that our "hunt for

God" might take time, I packed a sack lunch of our favorite foods: peanut butter sandwiches, chocolate chip cookies, and pretzels. Arriving at the park we decided to put first things first—we ate lunch.

"Have you found God here before?" I asked as we chomped on our cookies.

"I've never been here before," Josh told me.

"How do you know God is here, then?"

"I just know," he said with confidence.

"Well then," I said with a smile, "let me know when you spot God."

Josh began his search and I watched with fascination. He hugged a dog, stepped in a puddle, rolled down the hill, twirled around and around, ate another cookie, sat on the bench watching the bigger kids play ... and through it all, he giggled, and giggled, and giggled. Whenever I came close to him, I heard him through his giggling, repeating over and over, "I found God." Gradually, throughout the afternoon, I started to see the park I had visited many times with new eyes. That day, Josh, in his innocence, wisdom and delight, gave me a new perspective about God.

And so I began my own journey of looking for God in Iraq. As I now tell these stories, not knowing the future of this unsettled area, I have purposed to change most names.

JOURNEY TO IRAQ—
"IN YOU I TRUST"

"There are no feelings we feel that others have not felt before. At such times we unite ourselves with those who came before us."

Each time as I travel to unsettled parts of the world I feel a sense of kinship to the many who have experienced a similar adrenaline rush. Feelings become vivid. Fear and excitement merge, probably much like a mountain climber facing a sheer cliff. As I review journal notes recording the beginnings of my journey to Iraq, I see and again feel this type of unity with others.

I had heard of roadside and suicide bombs, the widespread hatred between factions in Iraq and its consequent destruction, and now the huge animosity of many toward the invading Americans. I especially also wondered about tales I had heard about inexplicable goodness.

This trip's purpose was to train Iraqi doctors and nurses in emergency medicine in medically isolated northern Iraq, an area of huge conflict. Eighty percent of its villages were destroyed. Nearly one hundred thousand to two hundred thousand of its people were killed through gas warfare carried out by Sadaam Hussein's forces.

Journal, September 15, 2003

Klamath Falls airport, 1640. Checked in a large bag. They searched it. Jo, my wife, detoured back home to get my handheld computer charger. Wonder if I will need it? Lots of things have been going on in my mind. Certainly this trip warrants thought. What is my purpose?

"God, I hope to show a bit of Your great love. I think the problems of this world are too immense for any other way to succeed. Help me do a good job. Give me an agile mind. May I be a good encourager. Bless my wife and care for her. It is so remarkable that she is willing to release me to You."

While waiting, I met Steve, who went to school with my son Noel. As a physician I took care of Steve's dad. Good memories. Steve's son, an eighteen-year-old, is leaving today to be in the military—a handsome lad. Are his feelings and mine similar?

Jo returned, put the charger in my carry-on. Time to go. A sweet kiss. Bye, honey! Lots of inner feelings! Homesick and haven't even left yet.

Journal, September 15 at 1725

Went through the initial boarding rigmarole and am waiting with my boarding pass in my shirt pocket. A large sober-appearing man sitting nearby is very pale and appears depressed. He speaks with a hoarse whisper to an attendant, and as he leaves for the plane he walks slowly, dragging his left foot. I automatically sift through my medical differential and all that I find is not good. He also faces immense obstacles. "Lord God, may he know your love."

Journal, September 16

Met my family, (daughter Jeanne, son-in-law Ted, and grandson Luke) at the Portland airport last evening without difficulty in spite of arriving a bit earlier than I expected. Had an excellent rest at their place and a good trip back into Portland with my nephew, Ron. Ron has lived a life of challenge and adventure working in many parts of the world with Medical Teams International (MTI). We talked, and I got lots of updating about positive happenings in the Middle East, Central Asia, Vietnam, and Latin America.

As a group leader, I spent time with Kristen at the MTI headquarters reviewing the plans, journey, and financing, and received packets of essential papers for each one in our group. Some will be given to the others in the group—I will keep some as backups. Planning in regard to our bags and what will be allowed involves taking CPR practice mannequins, defibrillators to restart hearts, airway intubation equipment to augment breathing, and much more. Needs are complex.

All of the group are very experienced in emergency medicine. Walking into the waiting area at the Portland airport with my carry-on bags, I met blond Valerie, an emergency room nurse from near Los Angeles; Ken Jr., a longtime, athletic-appearing paramedic from Portland; and Dr. Matt, a kindly emergency room physician from Tillamook, Oregon. Matt will be in charge of our training classes. I handed each their packet. Otto, a past paramedic and now an emergency room nurse from Tillamook, went on an earlier flight today, and we will join him in Istanbul, Turkey. It will be an excellent group with which to travel and work.

My favorite parts of these trips include the people I meet while traveling, and what I see of our beautiful Earth far below. However, most of this airline trip took place at night, so I missed seeing Greenland, icebergs floating in the North Atlantic, and the majestic volcanic peaks of Iceland.

Journal, September 17

Had a good flight to Istanbul, Turkey, via Frankfurt, Germany. The man I sat by from Portland to Frankfurt was a nontalker. I finally realized that he really didn't know English. He also seemed exhausted. So I quietly prayed for him, and by the end of the trip he had slept most of the way, was looking out the window some, and we exchanged smiles several times. "Lord, bless him and continue to touch him as You know best."

From Frankfurt to Istanbul I sat by a man from New Jersey. He had taught English as a second language thirty years before while in the Peace Corps in Turkey. He is only now returning for a visit and wonders about the changes he will see. As we landed at Ataturk

Airport near Istanbul he remarked, "It certainly looks different: many more buildings, a larger variety of airlines, more planes, and much busier appearing than thirty years ago." He seemed kindly, and we had a good time conversing about how it was thirty years before. "Lord, may he be touched and blessed by You."

Ara, who I knew from my earthquake days in Turkey, and Otto met us at the airport, and we journeyed to the Raddisson Airport Hotel. We made plans with Ara, a very tall, slender fellow who has played both amateur and pro basketball in and for Turkey. He will be our guide on our return through Istanbul. We exchanged e-mail addresses and will make contact before coming back out of Iraq. He is a kind fellow with a good sense of humor. His nickname for me is "Uncle Ken." The group enjoys him.

Journal, September 18 (Early morning)

Slept well. I had a good time sharing a room with Ken Jr. This morning we talked a bunch, prayed, and he read Psalms 25. It starts like this: "To You, O Lord, I lift up my soul; in You I trust." Superb!

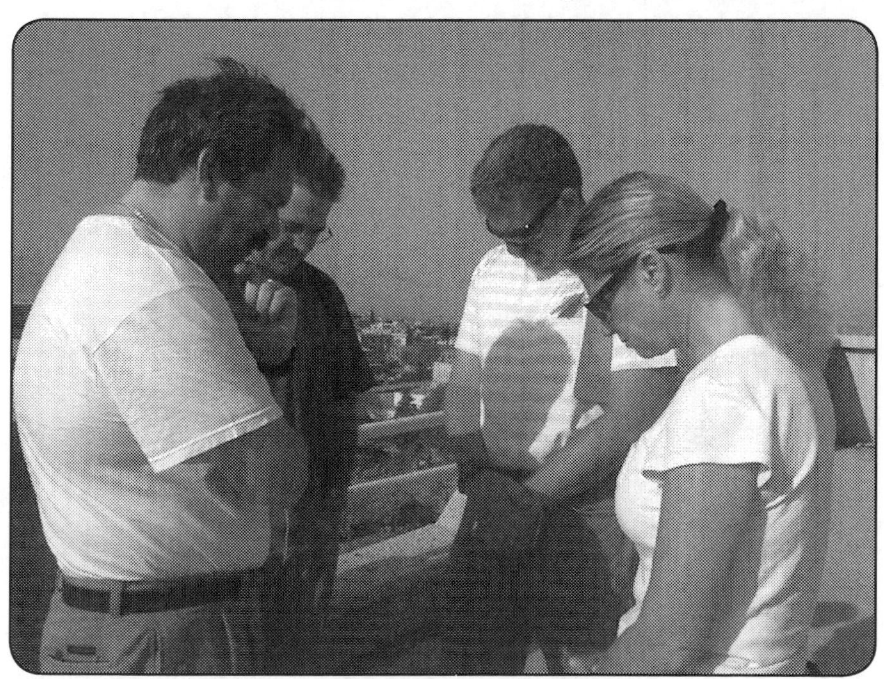

Journal, September 18, 1130

What a morning! The taxi drivers were slow getting our multiple bags loaded in their two cars. These autos are small, and the eleven bags are *big*—plus carry-ons. (As time slipped away, I found in myself a lot of inner anxiety. Two of our group, Val and Matt, had waited to be picked up later because of the lack of taxi room. The driver took us to the wrong terminal (international rather than domestic), and we unknowingly checked in there. Because of all the medical equipment, going through the detectors, scanners, and searches, the *slow* process was magnified.

By the time this was done, and we found it was not the correct terminal, our three hours of leeway time had melted away. When we finally pushed heavy-laden carts a lengthy distance to the domestic flights terminal and up to the counter with our eleven check-in bags, there was no sign of Valerie or Matt. I hurried back to where the taxis left us. Not there. We returned to the domestic terminal. Not there. We knew we'd best not try to check in with so many bags—not knowing where the others were. Our very exact plan with its multiple times to meet people and to be at predetermined places appeared totally fractured. My anxiety increased.

As our boarding time expired, Matt and Valerie appeared—from off the plane. They likewise were wondering and looking for us, then finally deplaned. We were too late for the flight to Diyarbakir in eastern Turkey. So we went to another ticket counter and were able to reroute a flight later in the day through Ankara that would get into Diyarbakir late that same day. People were very kind to us in that airport and charged us much less than they might have done for making these changes ($90 rather than $450). We were thankful and told them so. We dozed and waited for THY 412 to Diyarbakir via Ankara. We were in a pretty unoccupied waiting area, and most of the crew stretched out and slept. I leaned back. Glad I didn't topple over.

As it turned out, our departure from Istanbul was very delayed. After boarding, the plane just sat there for an hour before takeoff. With only a half-hour of leeway in Ankara, we knew we would miss our next plane. The hotel in Diyarbakir expected us that night, then a van was to pick us up early in the morning and drive us four or five hours to Silopi, on the Iraqi border. There, a man was to meet us and arrange taxis for crossing through the eight checkpoints into Iraq, where translators and drivers were to meet us at the "Tea House." Our plans appeared a mess.

Deplaning in Ankara, we hurried into the terminal and were surprised to find the connecting flight had also been detained. We'd experienced a lot of needless worry.

Trust—King David validated this through experience long ago. I've got a lot to learn.

We did reach Diyarbakir, "the walled city," that evening. After checking into the Hotel Class, we took a brisk walk down the crowded street to visit the giant dark basalt wall that surrounds the city. It dates back hundreds of years. Much of it is intact, some is broken down, and some has been repaired. Huge towers interrupt the wall periodically. I was impressed by the large blocks of basalt. How did they manage to cut them so many hundreds of years before? We followed it for about three hundred meters then turned back to our busy street. Some feel this wall is second only to the Great Wall of China.

Not only was the street lined with small shops, but many vendors with their carts bargained with customers. Watermelons, colorful heaps of citrus fruit, and small golden delicious apples were alluring. Colorful fabrics that would intrigue my wife were in some shop entryways. (In fact, later on my return, I purchased three yards of a deep purple material for my wife.)

After exploring the Hotel Class (we found a sitting room lined with bright yellow, green, red, and blue cushions and a lovely swimming pool), eating dinner, and a good night's rest, early the next morning Ken Jr. (so dubbed for being the younger Ken) and I again took a quick walk down the street. At this hour it was mostly vacant of carts and people but awakening as we returned to the hotel.

I stopped in an Internet cafe to send a message home. After sending it I paid the young proprietor, and he advised me to be sure and put my change back into hiding before leaving. A member of a previous team had had his pockets picked on this same street, so we all were careful to have our valuables tucked in belts close to our skin. For me it was important to remember that this wasn't Klamath Falls.

Journal, September 19

Having gotten up early we were ready when the van came to our Diyarbakir hotel to transport us to the small town of Silapi, near the border of Iraq. It was good to have a large vehicle and to not worry about multiple taxis for all our bags and six people.

The countryside in eastern Turkey had some mountainous areas, with flat country stretching to the west and south. A few scattered trees, about the size and shape of our junipers at home, speckled the hillsides. Frequent flocks of sheep and goats (usually accompanied by a man or youth on a donkey) searched the countryside for food. The grass and stubble appeared mostly yellow and endlessly grazed. Black goats were scattered about, but the multicolored sheep seemed to prefer closeness, staying in small flocks. When we passed near them we could hear their bleats and occasionally got a whiff of their feed yard smell.

The fields were narrow and long. I wondered why. Crops, probably mostly grain, had been removed, and field burning was common. Here and there large mounds, rising out of the floodplain, bore adobe brick and rock houses forming unpretentious villages. I wondered at the history buried under each town.

Our journey skirted the Syrian border, where cement posts held many strands of razor wire. About one hundred meters behind this fence was another fence and frequently spaced guardhouses resting on stilts. Numerous armored vehicles and groups of armed troops made us increasingly aware of tensions felt by the Turkish military as we neared the Iraqi border.

BORDER CROSSING SURPRISES

Nearing Iraq, I was surprised by the Tigris River and its beauty as it formed the divide between Syria and Turkey. I had not expected such clear blue water in a wide but rapidly flowing stream. Shrubs with red and green leaves and birch-like trees buttress its edges. We began to see areas of flood irrigation with some green fields. We saw cotton bolls nearly ready for plucking. Craggy peaks, footmen of Mount Ararat, rose to the north as we approached the Iraq border.

My diary next records the following:

September 19, Silopi, Turkey—It was early afternoon when our van pulled into this little border town. We were given instructions that someone would meet us there and help transfer our baggage to waiting taxis. Our driver, who seemed most pleasant but didn't speak English, turned the van into a walled vacant lot, where a dozen or more taxis were parked. Their competing drivers crowded around us, speaking forcefully, wanting to load us immediately into their taxis. Some even grabbed luggage from the back of our van. Thankfully, our driver calmed the animated crowd and our anxiety, and seemed to indicate that we must just wait. Minutes later one man arrived who seemed to be in charge and in broken English told us we couldn't leave to cross the border for another hour. He took us to a small cafe about a block away, indicating we were to wait there. It did make for an opportunity to drink some tea, eat some tasty lamb, and take turns detouring to a nearby water closet with its squat toilet. (It was only later, on our return, that I understood the delay. The border closes down at noon for two hours each day.)

The "head man" came and got us at the end of the time period. Three taxis wait, loaded with our luggage. We hope it is all there.

At about 2:00 p.m. our three cars, stuffed with luggage, left Silopi for the border. I was in a car alone with my driver, while two of our group followed in each of the other taxis. Soon after starting, my driver abruptly pulled to the roadside and stopped. The other two taxis sped by and quickly disappeared in the distance. My cab driver got out and ran over to a nearby village area. With my comrades gone, and waiting there alone, I felt a bit uneasy, but he quickly returned with a liter of gasoline and poured it into the little yellow car's tank. All was well.

We drove on, passing two *long* lines of petroleum tanker trucks stretching four or five kilometers up to the border. The tankers were not moving. We saw drivers in small groups conversing, sitting and playing cards, or munching on snacks.

At our first checkpoint my driver caught up to and passed one of our cars. I wondered what had gone wrong. Why had it been detained?

It was a long process going through eight different border stations. Generally, this involved a lot of waiting before they inspected my papers and luggage, etc. Our good helpers in eastern Turkey, John and others, had notified the border authorities that we would be coming and informed us it would take anywhere from two to eight hours to get across. (After four experiences of crossing the border in and out of Afghanistan, I was not surprised.) One especially long wait resulted from time needed for those commanding a checkpoint to get back from lunch. My driver, who spoke almost no English, was able with gestures to let me know at each stop whether he should take my papers or if I should be the one to hand them over to the officials.

Uniformed guards asking questions and wielding official stamps at the various stations generally seemed bored, unsmiling, and certainly moved at their own pace—*slow*. Armed soldiers were frequent, and on the Turkish side of the border we saw a large military presence, including several armored vehicles.

Our bags at one point were placed on tables and opened. One bag carried a full-size human figure we call "Resuscitation Andy," naked from the waist up. As one guard unzipped it, his and his partner's eyes widened in surprise. They stepped back. One hurried to get his superior. We attempted to explain, and thankfully they quickly understood. We all had a good chuckle together.

At another checkpoint one of the guards drew out a small picture to show us. It was a copy of a plane smashing into the World Trade Center on September 11. I'm sure our expressions were serious and one of our group said, "It makes us sad." Several guards stood around watching what our reaction would be. They seemed disappointed.

Finally reaching the last of eight checkpoints, the two of our group who had trailed caught up with us. There I heard the story of why my driver passed them at the first checkpoint. The Turkish guards were concerned about a digital camera, seized it, and made them erase any pictures taken near the border crossing. We were learning.

Leaving that last checkpoint, my friendly taxi driver announced with a big smile, "Welcome to Kurdistan." Only later did I fully understand the large implications of his statement. He drove me on to the "Tea House," where we five relieved Americans disembarked. We were warmly greeted by those who would help us in-country, and began swapping stories. The border crossing had only been a three-hour event, nothing like the two weeks our initial group from Medical Teams International experienced in entering Iraq.

(When we returned through this border three weeks later, I saw this same young taxi driver. He rushed over to me and gave an eager smile and handshake as though I was his long-lost friend. I relished his warmth.)

THE TEA HOUSE—WONDERINGS

The "Tea House" yet makes me wonder. Julio and Nawzad, who would be in charge of logistics, hurried us up the broad steps at the back of the house to its second floor. We opened a door on the small upper-level porch and entered an almost barren room except for several men who sat conversing in low voices. Their talking stopped, and I felt stares as we passed through to another smaller sitting room. In spite of having seen many people crossing the border at the various Turkish checkpoints, we appeared to be the only travelers here. Why so many seemingly idle men? Or was I seeing only a veil?

Two drivers, Dlawar and Mosoo, had been assigned to transport us to the city of Irbil. I felt lifted by their obvious warmth. After greetings, they hurried to transfer our luggage to the two waiting cars. The afternoon was being consumed, and we received advice that we needed to hustle in order to get through Mosul, an unsafe area, before dark.

An Iraqi gentleman who seemed in charge at the Tea House asked to take our passports. I felt reluctance in letting mine pass out of sight, but Julio reassured us that this was standard procedure and needed to be done. I was glad that I had copies of not only my own, but all of the team's passports carried in a belt next to my skin. The Iraqi man soon returned, having made a record of our names and passport numbers. The passports had not been stamped, and no visas were issued. The bureaucratic complexities of a more stable government had not yet developed.

Hurrying to exit this border area, we were slowed by long lines of large, eighteen-wheel oil tankers waiting to enter Turkey with crude oil and gasoline. Several nearby fields were crowded with halted trucks. I wondered how many days some might wait. According to our odometer the lineup extended over four kilometers.

Travel from the border to Irbil would take about three hours. We hurried through generally flat countryside and low rolling hills, both covered by yellowed grass or stubble of grain fields. Flocks of variously colored sheep and black goats searched for food throughout these low hills. Frequently we saw movable shepherds' homes covered by tented black roofs of carefully woven mohair. In one area of higher hills capped with rocky outcroppings, vineyards and fields of melons crowded into small valleys. Grapevines did not cling to wires, as is usual in our country, but stretched their branches outward and downward in a circle to the sandy soil.

My diary describes this part of the further journey as follows:

The highway seems decent, and workmen in several areas are grading its surface and spreading asphalt. Mosul, ancient Ninevah, incites our particular interest. Its huge walls, now mostly towering ridges of eroded soil and rock, extend for many kilometers. In some areas the wall and gates are being repaired.

Passing a large upscale area behind high walls we are advised, "This is where Saddam Hussein's sons died. Mosul is not yet a safe area for Americans. To be caught in a traffic jam of hostile people could be fatal."

We skirt the northern edge of the city to avoid downtown congestion and at one point briefly follow three American Bradley Fighting Vehicles. On each, above armored plates covered with shades of tan and brown, perches a single soldier, his machine gun searching the nearby streets. I am struck by the youth of the soldier on the closest unit—such responsibility for one so young. We wave, and he waves back. A Blackhawk helicopter flits across the sky above.

(A week later another American soldier was killed in Mosul. *I wondered if …*)

The highway led us northeast toward Irbil, where we learned a suicide bomber had blown himself up only a few days previously. Entering an area regulated by Kurds, we came to the remnants of a cement bridge spanning a large stream. It had been demolished by Saddam's forces. Perhaps they were expecting attacks from the Kurdish-controlled areas. Our cars proceeded cautiously across a steel replacement erected by US forces.

Near the bridge we stopped at a roadside stand to buy some soft drinks and stretch our legs. A young man and two boys came by with their burro. It made a good opportunity to snap some pictures, including one of Ken Jr. crowning the burro's forehead with a paramedic patch.

Shadows creeping eastward companioned us as we continued toward Irbil, and ultimately dusk arrived. Finally, at a busy junction we merged with a variety of little-controlled traffic, including an occasional donkey-drawn cart. There an imposing green sign indicated the way to the right could carry one to Kirkuk and Baghdad. What unknown experiences awaited us just ahead in the ancient city of Irbil?

IRBIL CLASSES—ADVANCED CARDIAC LIFE SUPPORT

A pair of armed guards met us in front of a queue of rock-filled yellow oil barrels, closely spaced to obstruct the roadway into the Chwar Hotel in Irbil. A high wall of cement blocks protected the wide front lawn from a busy street. We saw scattered tables surrounded by hotel guests from many countries, most engaged in earnest conversation, and some chuckling together. This large area extended back to our temporary home of five floors. Slinging straps over our shoulders, we carried our personal luggage up the broad front walk, passing the seated guests. It became our privilege in future evenings to join with this very international assembly. As we entered the hotel, our drivers, along with Julio and Nawzad, the in-country logisticians, drove off, transporting the medical bags to Medical Teams International's headquarters.

Two desk clerks anticipated our group and furnished each of us with a key to five adjacent rooms on the fourth floor. My room had two single beds. Recalling that several hotels in Iraq had been badly damaged from explosions, I chose the bed farthest from the windows. During several nights in this hotel I only heard nearby gunfire on one occasion. I slept well.

Our next two days were consumed with unpacking and organizing the equipment for classes, meeting with the deputy minister of health, and conferring with Dr. Barzani, the teaching hospital's director. Their greetings radiated warmth and grace and were always completed with tea. As we toured Rizgary Hospital we became increasingly aware of the difficulties of the last twenty years. Rizgary means "salvation." The hospital had formerly been named "Saddam Hussein Hospital." It lacked up-to-date equipment and many medications. An old CT scanner was inoperable. Otherwise, it appeared very clean and well kept.

In spare moments during those two days, I reviewed the areas of teaching that would be my responsibility: acute coronary syndromes (heart attacks), medications used in advanced cardiac life support (ACLS), and unstable supraventricular tachycardias (rapid rhythms originating in the upper parts of the heart, the atria).

Our team proved to be a well-chosen group. Ron of MTI had initially planned the venture and was to be team leader. Because of his intense responsibilities in developing a group headed soon for Vietnam, I drew the short straw as the replacement with the most prior experience in such ventures. Dr. Matt did a superb job as our curriculum leader.

Matt is an emergency room physician who grew up in a physician's family, studied and worked as an RN for several years, then returned to medical school, followed by a residency in emergency medicine. Matt is a kind "people person" with a keen memory and is most astute with computers. When questioned by Iraqi doctors, he ably gave them excellent up-to-date information in a manner that affirmed them as our equals. He helped me and others refine our PowerPoint presentations and produced an outstanding program on his laptop summarizing our trip for use in expositions on our return home.

Otto fled Cuba as a three-year-old child, brought by his family. This was only the start of an adventurous life. Escapades as a youth later calmed into activities such as mountain climbing, long stints of hard work on fishing boats in the Pacific Ocean, marketing seafood, and, finally, working as a paramedic in east Los Angeles. Otto then returned to school to become an emergency room nurse. His bright mind, sense of humor, and love of adventure certainly equipped him well for his present work. He compiled his own small glossary of Kurdish words and phrases. I envied his keen mind in grasping the language.

Valerie, an emergency room nurse from near Los Angeles, was experienced in teaching ACLS courses and had also worked extensively in prisons. Valerie has had a fascinating life, though not easy. If I were to pick two words to best describe her they would be "profound determination." Valerie tried vigorously to gain access into an active prison in northern Iraq. She was met with many excuses. On our last day in Irbil, she was promised a tour of the prison's infirmary and was told to arrive soon after noon. At the proposed time, our driver pulled into a narrow driveway surrounded by high adobe walls topped by razor wire. Our interpreter told the two guards at the outer gate of our arrangement, and one of them left briefly to speak with his commandant. Quickly he returned to inform us that, "You should have come this morning. We cannot now let you in." Gifted with a little more time, I'd bet Valerie would have succeeded in gaining entry.

Valerie strengthened the role of women in a part of the world where they are often considered less capable. Her teaching was excellent and was accepted well by all but one of the male doctors.

Ken Jr., a paramedic from Portland, Oregon, with years of experience, is most proficient at his business. He has faced monumental personal challenges. Perhaps this is why he is so gifted in loving people. It is his way of being a Christ follower. The nurses and physicians attending his intubation classes loved both him and his calm and enthusiastic approach.

What a good group with which to work. All most capable and representing the wisdom of years. All filled with compassion for hurting people. Each one closely attached to family "back home."

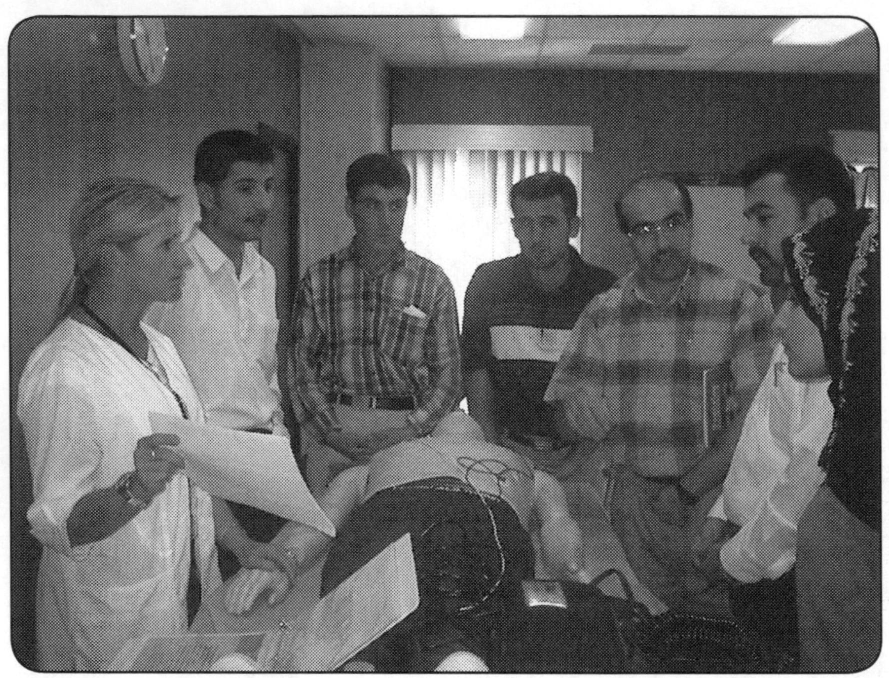

Dr. Barzani greeted us again on our first teaching day along with twenty-five eager Iraqi physicians and nurses. Their enthusiasm multiplied as the week progressed. We were sorry we could not accommodate other medical personnel who asked to be included. Several medical school classes came by to observe. Through our lectures, demonstrations, and then hands-on practice, it was our intent to train physicians and nurses who would then in turn be able to conduct further advanced cardiac life support classes.

After a week of teaching, I recorded the following:

Journal, September 26, 2003—Time passes so quickly. It is amazing. We concluded our first week of classes today. Totally successful. When starting, I felt apprehensive but also well-prepared. Had lots of help from Above.

At the graduation, the teaching hospital director, Dr. Barzani, and also the deputy minister of health from this part of northern Iraq gave brief talks. Expressing thanks for what had happened, they seem hopeful of continuing such educational involvement in the future. Then Julio, Matt, Valerie, Ken, Otto, and I each spoke. Afterward, Otto remarked, "I like to talk, but it sure makes me uneasy to give speeches."

We took turns handing out certificates to each one completing the classes. As we shook the hands of those friendly faces, I silently prayed for them. I wondered what the future holds. There is enormous stress and uncertainty in their lives, but now there is also increased hope.

We journeyed on to Salaimania following our time in Erbil and stayed in a hotel while conducting further emergency medical training in a nearby hospital. Each evening we gathered for a time with others at tables on the wide lawn to eat kebabs of lamb or chicken and flat bread, and to consume Fanta, an orange soda. It afforded opportunity to relax, to talk both business and fun, and to meet many others of widely varied backgrounds.

One of those was a huge, tall, and well-built Dutchman, "in Iraq on business." He related especially well to Otto. They have had similar lives of daring—on the high seas, mountain climbing, etc. He obviously loved Otto's bounteous sense of humor, which Otto blames on his Cuban heritage. The Dutchman always seemed to gravitate toward our group. We enjoyed his company. He told us about entering Iraq in a short convoy and being fired upon. A lady in the car following his was killed.

Three middle-aged American men sat at a small table conversing. They had small packs and satchels. We introduced ourselves and asked what they were about. One stated, "We are teachers." They appeared reluctant to say more. A day later we observed them leaving. They carried sidearms and small automatic rifles even though dressed in civilian clothes.

I met Abdulwahab Alkebsi in our Salaimania hotel lobby, where we'd both gone to find a breakfast of bread, cheese, juice, and a boiled egg. He smiled graciously and seemed to enjoy conversation. He is the program officer for the Middle East and North Africa, working for the National Endowment for Democracy, an American organization. Their objective is to encourage and support freedom around the world. Abdulwahab seems an energetic optimist who sought groups in Iraq to encourage. Their financial backing is intended to help such groups succeed and become independent of ongoing help. He stated that prominent people from across the political spectrum in the United States support this effort.

Each evening, several scrawny feral cats flitted in and out from under the surrounding bushes hoping for bits of kebab or bread. Their plaintive cries reminded us that life is indeed very difficult for many in Iraq.

THE STORY OF MILLENIUM

Sabri's husband served as part of the Peshmerga—"Those who face death." He had operated with others in the hills near Kirkuk opposing the advance of Saddam's army. There had been no word for many weeks, and then finally Sabri learned, with the arrival of a wounded comrade, of their unit skirmishing violently with the enemy. This was two years ago. Since then, the ongoing silence was heart-splitting. Hope vanished. A little girl had been born three months after Sabri's husband disappeared.

Life overflowed with difficulties. Sabri could neither read nor write. Had it not been for family and friends in her little village near Irbil, she and her baby would have died. She often sobbed through the night. A friend told Sabri of a group called Millenium in Irbil. They trained single mothers and widows who had no education how to read and write, as well as how to add and subtract numbers. They also taught these suffering ones how to make simple articles to sell and how to shop in the markets. Sorrowfully, Sabri left her tiny daughter with a sister and journeyed into Irbil. This was where I visited her and others.

Our small van turned into a short lane bounded by uneven walls of cement blocks. I bent forward, squinting to try to read the sign at the end of this alley. It was shadowed by the branches of a tree. Part appeared inscribed in Kurdish and part in English. After alighting and walking up the short roadway we could see it more clearly announcing, "Millenium, Helping Hands Program, Gilkand

Center for Women Activities, Millenium and Northwest Medical Services." We moved toward the doorway of the simple single-story house with the happy anticipation of getting to visit this training center for microeconomics.

A smiling lady with glasses and black hair coiled in a bun greeted our group at the doorway. She appeared to be in her thirties and wore a lavender blouse decorated with lighter-colored flowers and a dark purple skirt with hemline near her ankles. She greeted us warmly. As she shook hands with each of us she said, "I am Maurelia, the supervisor of this training center. This is my son." Her small son, wide-eyed, squatted nearby. After introductions she related a bit of her own history. Nearly six years previously she had traveled from her home in Costa Rica to work with these widows of northern Iraq. In her years of teaching, she recounted not only learning the Kurdish tongue herself, but with the help of others brought literacy and knowledge of ways to earn a simple living to about one thousand women.

Entering a small room we discovered a young Iraqi lady, her hair concealed by a light blue headscarf, working at a sewing machine. She was creating beautiful miniature flags of Kurdistan. A small glance and smile came our way, and then she continued on with her task. Completed flags and other products, including many colorfully dressed Iraqi dolls, rested on a nearby shelf ready for sale.

In the next room we found eight young women creating these dolls and dressing them in typical Kurdish clothes. The little doll men wore turbans colored and patterned to denote their family background, baggy shirts and pants, and encircling sashes at their waists. Each lady doll had her head covered with a scarf, while wearing a long, colorful dress with pantaloons peeking out at her ankles. A colorful sash encompassed each waist.

Their assembly line began with one Iraqi woman cutting old cloth into tiny pieces for stuffing and progressed to others sewing arms, legs, torsos and heads, and finally two who were drawing faces and gluing hair on those tiny heads.

Black tresses on the girl dolls certainly matched the human hair of their creators. *I wondered.* Two more women were busily sewing by hand, producing the miniature Kurdish garments and dressing the dolls.

Five chattering women in the next room briskly sewed quilt blocks together. These blocks displayed large flowers depicting the national flower of Kurdistan. It would be a gorgeous quilt.

We sensed a faint scent of lilies upon entering the next room. Smiling ladies looked up. They sat at tables making artificial flowers, greeting cards, and clothing. Most of the clothing these students wore had been fashioned as part of their training.

Knowing we were health-care workers, Maurelia pointed out Sabri and asked me to see her. This widow suffered from painful urination and frequently had to leave her work to go to the water closet. Maurelia motioned Sabri aside. I asked more questions, with Maurelia interpreting. Sabri had no money to see a doctor or to buy medicine. My personal kit at our hotel held just the medicine she needed. I arranged to send this medication back with one of our drivers.

Before we left, Maurelia described the earlier story of Sabri's becoming a widow and the ensuing destitution. As I glanced about that room, thoughts were stirred: *Most of these single women, nearly all mothers, could tell similar stories of fear, screams, grief, and despondency. Life remained difficult but now hope also grew.*

And Maurelia looked like such an ordinary person. What had prompted her to travel from her home in Costa Rica to the other side of the world, where danger to herself and her family prowled close at hand? Her smile radiated peace and kindness. She did not talk like, or appear to be, a lunatic.

DR. AHMAD'S COMPASSION

As Dr. Matt and I followed the long white coat of Dr. Ahmad into the small cardiopulmonary resuscitation practice room, I was struck by a faint but familiar odor sometimes associated with advanced illness. Across the room from Resuscitation Andy, our life-size practice mannequin, we saw Dr. Ahmad's patient supported with pillows on a couch-like bench. She appeared much older than her thirty-two years. Her eyes and cheeks were sunken, and her lips were blue. She exuded impending death.

It was common while in Iraq for the two of us to consult on patients with especially difficult predicaments. We also attended and participated in several early-morning meetings with groups of Iraqi doctors where problem patients were presented. With fresh hope in Iraq, we found intense enthusiasm for our input. Dr. Matt had been asked to see this particular lady, and he in turn requested that I join him.

Her name was Dashrah, and her sister, Bahar, hovered beside her. Dr. Ahmad, a middle-aged physician, had cared for Dashrah for about a year and, after introducing us, gave this history:

"When I first saw Dashrah a year ago, she was being helped slowly into my office complaining of chest pains and severe shortness of breath. Her blood pressure was elevated, but she also had much lung congestion and swollen legs. A chest x-ray revealed an enlarged heart and an aneurysm of her aortic arch, (an abnormally dilated and fragile ballooning of the large artery channeling blood away from her heart). She was in congestive heart failure. As you know, we have not had access to many medicines found in much of the world. I did start her on digoxin to strengthen her heart, furosemide to take off extra fluid, and potassium chloride to keep her potassium level stable because of the extra loss from her increased urine output. Dashrah did well. Her shortness of breath eased, and swelling disappeared. She became able to walk up a flight of steps again.

"However, after two months of seeming to do better," Dr. Ahmad explained, "she again began to deteriorate. I increased the medicines for fluid removal and watched her potassium closely. I fortunately was able to find and start captopril (a medicine that decreases obstruction in the circulation leading away from the heart). However, her situation became more complicated as her blood pressure became too low, and her kidney function began to deteriorate."

He went on to say, "Now, Dashrah is very short of breath and can only walk a few steps. In order to be able to breathe, she has to prop herself up with pillows. She cannot lie flat—not even for a minute."

While Dr. Ahmad was telling us the story he showed us a chest x-ray, holding it up against the light of the window. It displayed her very enlarged heart and the shadow of a grossly enlarged aorta just above her heart. An ECG (electrocardiogram) showed changes consistent with cardiac enlargement and a possible area of injury. An old type ultrasound confirmed very diffuse heart enlargement, extremely feeble contractions, severe leakage of the heart's mitral valve, and the abnormal aorta.

Both Dr. Matt and I took time to confirm by physical exam the sad saga that we had already heard. Dashrah's arms and legs appeared wasted, and her legs were severely swollen below the knees. Her bright blue blouse was embroidered with tiny flowers about the neck and down the front. Easing up its long tail, we found a young woman with no remaining body fat, only skin covering her conspicuous ribs—now appearing almost a skeleton. She had shallow breathing interspersed with frequent hungry gasps for air; even while sitting quietly, her lungs were filled with the sounds of fluid in their lower halves. My stethoscope transmitted a rapid heart rate and the swishing sound of a badly leaking mitral valve.

Dr. Ahmad's question to us: "What should I do?"

We reassured him that he had done very well with what little was then available in Iraq. Many medications that might potentially help were not obtainable. They had no means of further evaluation such as newer ultrasounds or angiography (dye studies of the heart's arteries). What had been a referral center in Baghdad was now in turmoil, and transferring her out of country seemed impossible. In fact, she was probably beyond the possibility of a heart transplant or other large intervention, even under the best of circumstances. Not even continuous home oxygen existed here in northern Iraq.

As Dr. Ahmad relayed our conclusions to the patient and her sister in their Kurdish tongue, we clearly saw his somber face. Tears brimmed his eyes. Dr. Matt and I felt the impact of this reality: *Here is a physician who has not only done the best possible under very hard circumstances, but deeply loves his patients. We believe Dashrah and Bahar felt it too.*

MEETING DERRICK

Someone said that he might be here. Entering the small room, I seated myself on the opposite side and then glanced about. The area was circled by humanitarian aid workers from many parts of the world. Across the space sat a slender graying man with tousled hair and deeply tanned arms and face, contrasting with a short-sleeved white shirt. As we introduced ourselves around the room, I could see a twinkle in his eyes and slight upward bend of the corners of his mouth. It was Derrick.

Derrick had been born in Germany and then while yet a lad migrated to the Netherlands with his family. I had heard bits and pieces about this exceptional man several years before.

His greeting and firm handshake communicated warmth. He had been told by a mutual friend in the West that I might be coming to Iraq. We agreed to meet and talk the following evening in a hotel dining room in Sulaimania.

While we enjoyed the flavor and smell of well-cooked lamb kabobs, Derrick recounted some of his past. Working as a television reporter for a European company he visited many parts of the world. Scenes deeply stirred him, including mothers begging for the lives of their diseased and starving children in Ethiopia, and boy soldiers in the Sudan learning to kill.

"I remembered the counsel of Christ to care for the poor, the hungry, and those in distress," Derrick recounted. "I progressively felt compelled to do more than simply film these tragedies."

Derrick's lips tightened, and his face was sober as he recalled, "And so I and my good wife, Gwen, determined to move to northern Iraq in 1991 to help as best we could. These people had suffered much; most villages had been destroyed, and their inhabitants became refugees lacking even the most basic necessities of life. The fighting left thousands of widows with children. Many of the little ones were starving. In attempting to better their lot, we found that illiteracy made feeding programs much more difficult. Most of the women from the villages could neither read nor write. Recognizing this huge poverty, we produced a literacy program for women in Iraq."

As Derrick proceeded with the story his voice was soft and exhibited an unmistakable gentleness even as he spoke of tragedy.

"One widow had six sons. When Saddam's forces came she was told, 'You may keep two of the boys. We will take the others.' Those four sons disappeared forever."

Derrick continued, "In addition to working to better the lot of women through literacy, we have also created a center where women here in Sulaimania can gather to talk and learn. It is very active. All of this helps to elevate their feelings of worth."

Several years ago, Derrick's wife, Gwen, suffered a severe headache and died of an apparent ruptured cerebral aneurysm. Derrick told me she is buried in a Muslim cemetery on a hill overlooking Sulaimania. They had wisely talked about such possibilities previously, and her wish had been to stay close to these people she loved dearly.

Derrick, burdened with overwhelming grief, returned to Holland for two years, where he struggled with deep depression. As it lifted, his former concern for this hurting people revived, and he returned to Iraq to lead his literacy program again.

Derrick related, "It is a privilege to live in this land of beginnings. The vast oil reserves attest to the rich vegetation once covering the area now desert. It is a land full of ancient history. What a wonderful land."

He went on to recount many of his convincements to me. "I hate war, but God can use tragedy if necessary." He feels that if the United Nations had indeed united in dealing with Saddam, peaceful solutions could have come about. "I hope this American effort is a success, not only for the sake of Iraq but also for surrounding countries. There are no free media in these countries. They can complain about the West but are not allowed to complain about their own countries. The formation of a constitution fair to all Iraqis is crucial. Pray for this to happen.

"There is no freedom, especially for women. A woman can't take a ride alone in a taxi in many of these countries. Men get together, but it is not easy for women to do. Women love to come to our Women's Center here in Sulaimania.

"But a lot of things are changing. There is a large movement toward freedom in nearby Iran. I hope America will give Iran time for these forces already at work, rather than hurriedly trying to impose freedom on them. Pray for peaceful change in Iran. Don't isolate them."

As we left the hotel restaurant to go our separate ways, Derrick again requested, "Please pray for all of these things."

I told him I would.

A few minutes later I stood alone on the hotel roof. To the west of Sulaimania, thick haze dimmed the horizon and colored the vanishing sun a deep red. Northward lay several city blocks in rubble from a past bombardment. Beyond on the grass-covered hills a few clumps of trees were visible in the fading light. One large area of grassland had been further blackened by a fire. I lingered for a long time and pondered the future for these dear people as darkness gradually deepened. Then among the flat-topped houses and along the streets below, lights began appearing, a few here and there, gradually increasing until there were many, and the city seemed alive.

NERGIS: PURSUED BY SADDAM HUSSEIN

"That night was probably one of the hardest It was the first time in my life I had really known fear."

Nergis sat across a small table from me relating some of her frightening past. I held a tiny tape recorder. During much of the last twenty years the forces of the Iraqi government had tried to destroy the Kurds of northern Iraq. Nergis had been trained as a nurse in a Western country, had most of her book work in English, and was easy to understand. She wore a long sky-blue dress and a light-brown vest and sash, with baggy golden pantaloons peeking out at her ankles. She had come to northern Iraq to work with starving children by teaching mothers how to prepare food for tiny ones and to promote literacy as a step toward health education. As she related some of her history, her face often appeared tense. At times her voice trembled slightly or faded until scarcely audible. This is her story in her words:

> Saddam Hussein was launching another offensive against the Kurds of northern Iraq. We were listening to the news. At about the same time planes struck Baghdad, making Saddam very angry, and he said, "Strike the foreigners. Anywhere you see them, kill them."

In my home city people were packing up, ready to run for their lives. Then things started to calm down and seemed okay. However, within two days, in the middle of the night, I was staying with one of my friends when her son came and said, "We have to leave *now*. We don't have time to wait."

I had talked with United Nations personnel the day before and asked if they could take me to the border of Turkey. They replied, "No. But we can take you to Arbil," which was the capital city of northern Iraq. I had heard it was under the control of the Iraqi government and told them, "I can't go there."

In the middle of the night my friends said, "We don't want to leave you here because it won't be safe for you. We are fearful. Come with us."

So we left in a little Passat. I sat in the front with my friend and her son, who drove. In the back were four men—all of us in something about the size of a Volkswagen Rabbit! We just started driving. As far as the eye could see, both in front and behind us, were cars. I asked, "Where are we going? What is the plan?"

"The plan, what plan?" was their response.

"What do you mean no plan?"

"We're just running away."

The countryside there was beautiful—water and trees and lovely hills. In fact, while we were running for our lives, I was asking my friend if she could bend down so I could reach my camera out the window and snap a picture of the gorgeous scenery. Isn't that crazy?

Well, we got to the border of Iran. It was very crowded with people wanting to get into Iran, but the border was closed. A barricade had been built across the narrow road. An ammunition-belt-draped

Iranian soldier holding a machine gun stood on top of a nearby rocky hill. He looked down on us as if saying, "Don't cross this border or else!" There was much confusion and anxiety.

I didn't know what to do. I felt like I was imposing on my friends. They were running for their lives, and now they had to worry about this silly foreigner. I felt really bad and told them, "I will just go back and try to get to the UN office somehow."

My friends didn't know what to do with me but reluctantly agreed. A few miles behind us lay a certain village where I could stay until morning. The only problem was that the vehicles going back toward this village were Kurdish army vehicles. They were headed toward the front line and would drop me off on the way. They put me in the back of an armored personnel carrier, and we went racing off as it was getting dark. I thought, *How in the world did I get here?*

Soldiers were sitting on both sides of the back of the personnel carrier, facing outward. In the middle on the top of the cab was a large machine gun with its gunner next to it. I sat on the very back by the tailgate. This trip through rugged, rocky mountains with scattered trees and clumps of brush seemed very long, though it probably lasted only a half hour. I was terribly frightened.

They finally dropped me off at the small town, and I didn't know if I could trust these village people or not. They were not my close friends and could have easily turned me over to the Iraqi government. But they were very good to me. They heated water for a bath and tried to get me to eat, but I couldn't. I was too nervous.

That night was probably one of the hardest—well, it was the first time in my life I had known extreme fear. Would I be recognized as a foreigner by Iraqi soldiers at checkpoints, captured, tortured, or even killed? I thought of my family and prayed, *Lord, I know that following you sometimes involves suffering and death. But for the sake of my mother, please let me go home and explain to her why in the world I am doing this*. I didn't sleep at all that night.

The next morning I tried to get a taxi back to Sulaimania to contact UN personnel. But no one would take me—no one, no one, *no one*! They were too afraid. What could I do? So I finally decided to go back to the border.

When I got there I met a Kurdish lady who had been keeping house and cooking for a close friend of mine. I recognized her smile, dark red blouse, baggy pantaloons, and multicolored head scarf. Together she and I had been learning to read and write Kurdish. She was like a sister. She just took me in her arms and said, "Don't worry about anything. If we die, we die together. I am never going to leave you now that I've found you. You know we are Kurds. People and nations have been trying to kill us for centuries, but we are still living. Somehow we have a way of getting out of things."

She gave me confidence. After talking with other refugees, they decided to put me in the back of a big truck, an English lorry, headed for remote mountains.

They put a scarf around my head, so I'd look just like one of them. The lorry was full of women and children. We sat with our knees pressed against our chins, unable to straighten our legs. We would take turns standing, but as you can imagine even that was very difficult in a moving vehicle on a rough road. The group included several very educated women I knew from the city, some with university degrees. It took us a long time to get to where we were going.

The first evening, after being in that condition for eight hours, we got out to use the bathroom. We didn't have toilet paper and had nothing to wash our hands. We had no drinking water, but some ladies offered me grapes.

I told them, "No, I want to wait until I can get someplace tonight where I can wash my hands."

One said, "Tonight? You think we are going to be somewhere tonight? If we get there by tomorrow night we will be very fortunate."

Standing there beside the lorry, I just started to cry, and everyone in the lorry became very concerned. Several rushed over to me. "What's wrong?"

We are packed in here just like animals, and you ask me, "What is wrong?" I thought, *You have done it so many times you don't even know what is wrong.* This made me cry even more. They were upset because they couldn't do anything about it, and really I was crying for them too. This was normalcy for them. I knew I needed to get control of myself for their sake, and I did.

We stopped at one place where, after introductions, I talked with a gentleman who tried to encourage me. He said, "Nergis, don't worry. If you live in the Middle East long enough, you will realize there is only one thing that is certain: that there is nothing that is certain. So this will change. Every situation changes. If it's bad, it can change for good."

That's really what happened. I was fortunate it only lasted a month. The great uncertainty and dealing with cold weather was difficult.

Finally we got to a safer place high in the mountains, which they said had never been touched

> by Saddam. His tanks were unable to traverse the narrow roads clinging to the sides of cliffs.

Nergis paused to sip some tea, and then she continued in a soft and thoughtful voice:

> That month was a very special time. I wouldn't trade that month for anything now. I know God had placed me there. It was not by accident or coincidence. He allowed me to experience just a very small part of the suffering my friends experienced in Iraq. I gained a deep love and respect for these people, and I have a great deal of favor with them because of this difficult time we endured together. They took good care of me. I believe I was sent there to encourage them to not lose heart by sharing with them my faith in a loving God, who will not allow injustice to continue forever.
>
> I helped start a small clinic in the mountains for the refugees. I took care of the women and the distribution of powdered milk, going to each tent that requested milk and actually preparing it with the mother so she would understand to use boiled water and clean glasses. This was such a rewarding time of getting close to the people.
>
> It was really beautiful there in the mountains, but getting food was difficult. Some went into Iran to try to bring back food. They were often stopped and delayed a week or two. We also tried to get word of our needs to the UN. The tents had hardly anything in them. There was no furniture. If they had blankets they would put them down on the ground to make a carpet. When I came into a tent, I took off my shoes. In some places they didn't even have a tent. They didn't have anything. When it started to rain

they would just huddle out under the trees. If they had a car, they would all pile into it. In one place where they had made a tent out of blankets, it caught fire. We had some extra tents by then and sent one of them over. These were often just sheets of plastic or canvas.

After a month the Kurdish soldiers were able to push Saddam's forces back, and I returned to the northern city where I started rebuilding my work. A large area had been destroyed in the center of the city, and the smell of decaying bodies and explosives lingered. I learned what it was like to begin again from nothing."

Nergis concluded her summary of these hard times with some hope for the future:

The people living in this region have built and rebuilt their lives many times. They have a lot of perseverance, and now they have some hope for the future. But they are also very tired.

When I was learning the Kurdish language, I learned that there are several past tenses, but no future tense verbs, at least not ones that are used in daily conversation. Present and future tense are the same. I think this says a lot about a people who have been very uncertain about the future. But I also learned something else from them. I learned how to make the most of and to enjoy the present.

GOD IS IN IRAQ

Tonight, six months later, I am looking at the picture sent by Ken Jr. of four of our physician friends in Iraq who are participating in the further teaching of ACLS courses in their country. Their felt presence is very real. It is a highly emotional time for me. "*Oh God, take good care of these dear men and all the families and people in that part of the world they represent. You know how intensely they hope for an end to violence and a better life ahead. I join them in that prayer.*"

(Though all this happened several years ago, names and places have been altered slightly for the safety of those yet living in Iraq.)

Kenneth K. Magee, MD

LIBERIA

Liberia was set up as a colony for former African American slaves in the early 1800s by citizens of the United States. Following the American Revolution there was a large upsurge of the movement to free slaves inspired by both some slaveholders and church groups. They began arriving in Liberia in 1821. Earlier it was known as the Pepper Coast because of the abundance of malegueta pepper. It was the home of numerous native tribes and more than twenty indigenous languages. The official language became English.

Initially they bought and settled in the area of present-day Monrovia but these Americo-Liberians did not identify well with the indigenous peoples. Conflict ensued. In 1824 it was named Liberia, with its capitol at Monrovia. In 1847 Liberia proclaimed itself a free republic and drew up a constitution similar to that of the United States, also denying voting rights to the native peoples. The Americo-Liberian 5 percent of the populace ruled the area, ever expanded their borders, and suppressed the 95 percent majority until the late 1900s. Much contention ensued.

However, between 1847 and 1980, Liberia expanded from simple agriculture to many exports of agricultural products—coffee, rice, palm oil and palm kernels, sugar cane, and hardwood timber. Firestone built the world's largest rubber plantation.

Terrible warfare followed in recent years, with most of the regal houses built by the former American slaves being burnt down. Conflicts arose with neighboring countries. The economy plummeted. A variety of leaders tried to gain and maintain supremacy, and finally the United Nations Security Council stepped in with peacekeepers. By then many of the people had fled to other countries or to IDP camps. It was into this hugely conflicted situation with its astronomical needs that Medical Teams International came in 2004, along with others, to give aid to a most ill people.

SINGE CAMP

"Dr. Ken, you needed quick outside. In a wheelbarrow be a man twisting from big pain."

My busy day at Singe IDP (internally displaced people) Camp for Liberian refugees was interrupted by an excited clinic helper. I had just started examining a wee baby held by her anxious mother. It was with a mixture of feelings that I left that little one with her difficulty breathing to follow the concerned clinic aide.

Our journey that morning had taken us over a long, muddy road interrupted by many deep pools. July is in the middle of Liberia's rainy season. I'm certain that dirty water would have poured in if we'd tried to open a door of our Land Cruiser. We got plenty of practice holding our breath expecting our engine to sputter and die. But the countryside was beautiful: magnificent trees and bushes of all sizes, including imposing "cotton trees," from which dugout canoes are shaped; palms crowned with clustered branches; groves of slender bamboo; and areas lavish with banana trees. Among the smaller bushes, some displayed bouquets of trumpet-shaped yellow flowers mounted on whorled leaves, and others flaunted enchanting lavender blossoms fit for a palace. Gorgeous!

We passed two other IDP camps before arriving at Singe. Many people were following along the roadway with bundles of leaves or branches or tubs of clothes on their heads. At two small streams others were busy washing clothes by pounding them on streamside rocks. Some were bathing in the streams. Rounding one corner we came upon a mother washing her young son, who was standing in a large basin of soapy water. He was covered with suds from head to feet. They both laughed and waved at us enthusiastically as our van slid by.

It was my first day to visit Singe camp. I wondered what we'd find. I quickly found out. The call to come immediately and visit the wheelbarrow was especially unforgettable.

Pressing through the waiting crowd we found four men with a wheelbarrow, its original red paint faded by rust and time. Two held its handles, and the others supported the passenger's extended legs. He wore a loosely fitting shirt and trousers, both the color of earth. Pain contorted and moistened his face. The man supporting his right leg was doing his best to hold it steady, but the slightest movement brought loud cries from the passenger.

His friends had wheeled him from the far side of the camp and related this story: "Two week before, Tomas be climbing up trunk of palm tree for cut and throw down branches to cover roofs. He be very high when he slip. He fall hard and have much pain here." He pointed toward Tomas's hip area. "We carry him to hut, and he be ona bed alla time."

The hip seemed to have no gross deformity, but even the slightest movement or palpation over the area caused intense discomfort. The leg was not perceptibly shortened or abnormally rotated. I concluded that although a fracture was almost certain, it was not badly displaced. I considered what to do. No x-ray unit was available in that area, nor was there an orthopedic surgeon, should repair be advisable. We gave him mild analgesics to take home, as nothing stronger was available, and instructed his friends that he be kept mostly in bed. They were told that I wanted to see Tomas again in four weeks.

(Nearly four weeks later I did see Tomas again. He had less pain and was able to move about with the aid of homemade crutches.)

I returned to the wee little girl. She had been treated for malaria a week before. Her mother said she was feeding from the breast well. Her anterior fontanelle, the soft spot in the front of her skull, was not sunken in, indicating no serious dehydration. A small area of moisture could be heard by stethoscope in one lung base. With her resistance lowered by malaria, bronchial pneumonia was the likely culprit. I ordered liquid antibiotics provided by our mobile pharmacy and prayed under my breath that the little one would do well. We would not be back for a week.

My coworkers, (Mary, an RN from Canada, and Sophia and Mildred, Liberian nurses from Monrovia), and I saw many children and adults that day. Mary found one young lady with severe respiratory distress due to bronchial asthma. Her efforts to both breathe in and breathe out were difficult. We were able to give little relief with theophylline and a small amount of adrenalin. Our supply of inhalers had been exhausted. She would need added help.

(Soon after this and with much effort Lorie, our in-country team coordinator, was able to procure more appropriate inhalers and corticosteroids.)

One young child with dysentery was very lethargic and had a dry mouth and sunken anterior fontanelle. She was no longer able to drink adequate fluids. Both she and the asthmatic lady would likely die without additional help. While she worked, Mary watched them closely, and at the end of the day we loaded both patients into our Toyota, along with the child's mother and a relative of the asthmatic lady, for transport to a small hospital in northwestern Monrovia staffed by a group of Doctors Without Borders. We were grateful for their help.

As our driver and medicine dispensers packed the top of the van with tables, chairs, and chests, a gathering of children from the surrounding tiny thatched-roof huts with walls of bamboo and mud, stood by to watch. Their faces revealed both curiosity and warmth. While waiting I was surprised by little fingers reaching up and grasping my right hand. Looking down I saw a beaming boy and smiled back. Another hand joined his and then another. Soon both my hands were full of tiny clinging fingers. I felt extremely stirred and realized that other Northwest Medical Team workers before us had surely done an excellent job of loving the little children of Singe Camp.

CAPTURED

Skeleton-size arms and legs dangled limply as his mother carried him to my small table. Flomo Nueto was my fourth patient at Kingsville Camp for Internally Displaced People in Liberia, right after the little girl named Surprise. As I pulled a thin blue and yellow blanket down from his chest, I saw his rapid but very shallow right-sided respiratory effort. Massive swellings bulged from both sides of his neck. As I took my light and with the help of a tongue blade looked in his dry mouth, his dull eyes opened. He did not whimper or protest. Death waited nearby.

Flomo had been brought by his mother and grandmother to this camp only a few weeks earlier. They had fled Lofa County, where the rebels had killed many people and where life was still a gamble. His father was gone. I could only imagine what had happened to him. Their escape had been a hard trip, full of grief. Flomo increasingly complained of "hot skin" and tiredness. In spite of the ministrations and loving care given by his mother and grandmother, he ate little and progressively weakened over three months.

The large neck masses were firm. My stethoscope found absent breath sounds in the left chest and crackles of moisture at the right lung base. My percussion of his chest walls intoned dullness on the left side. His left thorax was fluid-filled. Possibilities were several—mostly not good.

Hospitals in Monrovia, Liberia's capital city, had been devastated by the fourteen years of civil war. Now resources were extremely limited, and beds were few. We had been instructed to bring in from the camps only patients who would die without added help, but not to bring ones who would likely die anyway. My thoughts were weighted by the sudden death the night before of an eighteen-year-old hospital patient with severe heart inflammation. I talked with fellow team member Mary, from Canada, and decided to hospitalize Flomo.

His mother left her little son lying on a small bamboo bench and went down the path of slick red mud toward their tiny thatched hut—one among hundreds. She would gather a small plastic bag of necessities for them both. I kept an eye and an ear turned toward Flomo while a tiny white hen spent her morning scratching about in the dirt floor of the tiny room. Later that day, after seeing many other patients, we loaded the ailing boy and his mother in the back of our Toyota van for the trip to ELWA Hospital. Breathing rapidly, Flomo lay on his mother's lap. His twelve-year-old body looked much smaller than one would expect. I sat nearby and watched.

The following evening, after another busy working day, Mary and I returned to ELWA Hospital wondering what we would find. Flomo was alive! His left chest had a tiny needle mark surrounded by a large bruised area. Much fluid had been drained from the area surrounding his left lung by a Liberian doctor. He was being given IV fluids and antibiotics. He looked a bit better, and air was now moving in his left chest. I wondered what tests they had been able to run on the drained fluid and his blood. (I found later that they had been able to do a simple chest x-ray and indeed confirmed his left chest to be fluid-filled, which, under pressure, was pushing his heart to the right.) They concluded that tuberculosis was the likely culprit.

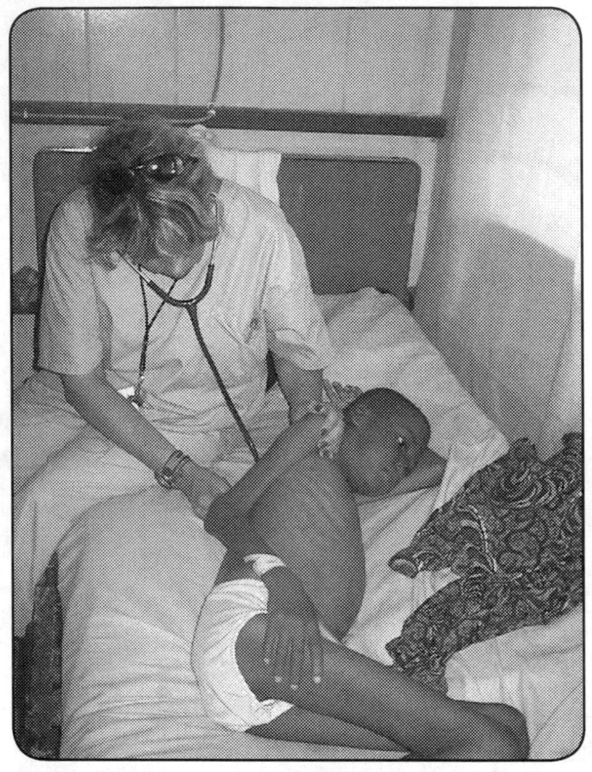

Flomo did get better. Soon, with each visit he repeated over and over, "Go with you? Go with you?" Mary did a grand job of encouraging his mother, and a week after admission they were ready for transport back to Kingsville camp. Flomo was eating, gaining strength, and walking. His lungs sounded remarkably better. He was given a month's supply of antituberculous meds (found with some difficulty). More were to be secured later.

As we departed, following the pathway down a gentle slope toward our waiting Land Cruiser, I felt a small hand reach up and grasp mine. With his mother following behind, Flomo and I walked together, hand in hand.

In subsequent IDP camp visits we saw Flomo several times. He continued to improve. On my last visit he stood outside a window cut in the blue tarpaulin walling of my tiny examining room and watched us most of the day. Sometimes, when privacy was needed, we would shoo him away for a bit. At the end of that last day he stood with the other children and waved as we left down the roadway of sticky red mud.

Oh God, do take care of Flomo. He captured my heart!

Dr. Bill, from Seattle, and I were able to procure five months more of antituberculous drugs, not then available in Liberia, and send them for Flomo. A half year later we heard from a nurse working there, "Flomo is doing well."

ENGLISH LESSONS IN LIBERIA

(From my journal, dated July 17, 2004)

Should I smile or frown? This is commonly my dilemma while listening to native fellow workers during travel to or from a refugee camp. The Liberian brand of English is so very different from mine. Spoken rapidly with many different inflections and pronunciations plus an unfamiliar use of words and phrases, it seems like a totally foreign tongue. So I just fake it. I watch Peter, our dependable driver, and try to proximate his expressions. But I also understand they know my quandary. When speaking directly to me they will slow way down, and after two or three tries we do communicate.

Medically I am fortunate to have interpreters to both deal with tribal languages and to help me understand Liberian English. Listen to some of these terms:

"How you keeping?" or "How the body?" is used for an opening question by the examiner.

"Skin be hot."—this is the presenting complaint of almost everyone. From there they go on to "Pee pee yellow," "Slimy stools," or "Stomach pain." Often the most important symptom is mentioned last.

"You can cough?" "You can put it out?" are the questions to ask when searching for sputum production.

"You are getting dry?" or "Is that your body?" are proper queries when checking for weight loss.

Heart palpitations are often described as, “Heart can be beating.”

Responses to an inquiry about pain also are sometimes confusing to my ears. The word for pain sounds almost exactly like “pee” to me. They might say, “Ah, all a body, pee, pee all over.” Can you understand my confused look?

“Have you eaten any food today?” may get a response such as, “No, I only swallow fufu,” (a thin gruel) or “No, I only drank tea.” To a Liberian, “food” means rice, so they may have eaten bread or other things.

“Pressure” generally refers to feelings they consider to be associated with high blood pressure, and is a common complaint. In fact I am struck by their lack of expressions for feelings, rather instead using somatic, or body, symptoms to describe anxiety, depression, or worry.

“Are you pregnant?” is asked by, “You got belly?” and, if there is a baby moving, by “The belly can shake?” It took me quite a while to understand the common term of “receive.” This refers to a lady’s period. When the complaint is, “I not receiving for three months,” I have come to finally realize a quick urine pregnancy test is usually appropriate.

I love their names. They remind me of names often given in our country many years ago, or ones connected to e-mails in present-day America. Of course, there is David and Daniel and Mary and Martha, just like we have in our culture. Here are some of the more intriguing ones:

Fineboy, Praise, Feeding, Othelo, Exodus, Baby, Partmor, Diamond, Saturday, Wayward, Ma (a tiny baby), Surprise, December, Passaway, Oma, Mama, Remember, Papa, T-Girl, Gift, Pinky, ZeZe, Lucky, To Tu Girl, God Gives, Blessing, Charity Monger, ST Living Stone, Younger Flomo, 1 (This tiny boy only had a number), Born Masu, Oldman Tomorrow (a baby), Mercy July, A.B. Charlie, God Knows, O-Kay, Small, Good Luck

Doesn’t this list fascinate you? I can only imagine that most interesting circumstances led to some of the naming.

IS THERE HOPE FOR LIBERIA?

From many mouths I heard these words: "This is Liberia's last chance." Not only did this statement come from people working with many NGOs (nongovernment organizations) and from those working through the United Nations to help bring back law and order, but many Liberians also expressed similar convictions. Fourteen years of civil war had left blackened cement skeletons of once magnificent homes and public buildings. Remaining buildings were covered by pockmarks of innumerable bullets. Roads typically are a maze of broken pavement, potholes, and mud with thick, crouching bushes along their margins. Wild birds and animals are rare in much of Liberia, having been killed for food. A railroad is long gone. Its bed is now providing gravel for roadways or paths of needy people. The crusher on Rock Hill in Paynesville is totally broken down. Now children and adults spend days hammering rock into gravel. They hope that somebody will buy it. The area called Red Light, like many areas, is lined with hundreds

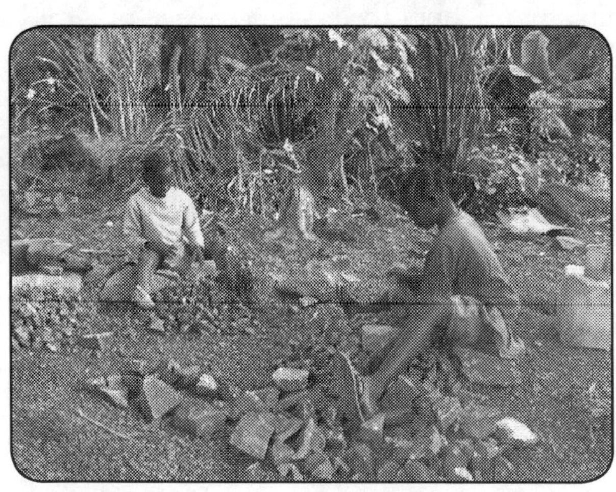

of tiny booths fashioned of bamboo, rusty castaway roofing, and other scraps from past devastation. Men, women, and youths tend these booths stacked with baskets, shoes, shirts, vegetables, and fruit, both guarding and hoping that at the day's end they will have something more for their families. Is there any reason for hope?

Everyone in Liberia seemed to have a difficult story produced by the years of warfare.

James gave me this account:

"Fourteen years ago, as a young teenager, I fled my home in Luiyeana, Luffa County. My dad was told a lie about being protected if he turned himself in to the rebels, after much of his own family had been killed. (He had been in the army.) Instead, they killed him and then came to kill other children in the family. I shut myself in the bathroom, and they overlooked me. As I fled I saw the body of my father floating facedown in the river. Later, four of my brothers tried to get revenge and were killed. I fled to Monrovia and haven't seen my mother since then. She was also probably killed. A family in Monrovia took me in, and I got to go on to high school."

I asked James, "What needs to happen?"

His answer: "Reconciliation. Even with my enemies. I hope many will take this path. It is the path of Christ."?

As Isaiah and I sat together on either side of a small oilcloth-covered kitchen table, we could smell the scent of the ocean and hear the nearby Atlantic surf. "Kitty," our young domestic cat, jumped up on the table and vigorously swatted at our hands, hoping to play or be petted. There in the small house rented by Medical Teams International and surrounded by many other houses pockmarked by bullets, Isaiah began this story and later wrote it in detail:

On August 10, 1977, I was born into the union of Mr. and Mrs. Isaiah C. Brown Sr. in a mining area near Yekepa, Nimba County. In 1981 I began my primary education at St. Joseph's Catholic School. A few years later my family moved to Monrovia, the capital of Liberia. I enrolled in St. Michael's Catholic School, where I remained for four successive years. My parents worked for the Liberian American Mining Company (LAMCO). I am the fourth of eight children who all grew up in this Christian home. In 1989 I was admitted into St. Patrick's Catholic School and attended this institution, with interruptions, until my graduation from high school in 1995. I was the valedictorian of my graduating class.

In 1990 a brutal and senseless uprising broke out in Liberia. This rebellion plunged the entire country into violence, thus bringing all normal activities to a virtual cessation. My family experienced a major tragedy during that period. On the fatal day of June 15, 1990, at precisely 11:45 p.m., my eldest brother and sister were forcibly taken out of our home by some unknown armed men and killed a few minutes later. May peace be to their souls. Though I was just thirteen, that horrible and terrifying scene still lingers in my mind. Many bloody areas nearby carried the stench of dismembered bodies, and I saw some floating in the river. Furthermore, my parents suffered constant intimidation and harassment from the hands of the rebels on the grounds that they were supporters of the incumbent government. That is untrue. My father worked for a private company. Violence pervaded the nation. Lawlessness, anarchy, murder, and other vices became the order of the day. Against this backdrop my family was forced to flee to Sierra Leone, a neighboring country, for safety of our lives. Thanks to the *Almighty*, we were able to survive.

We lived as refugees in Sierra Leone for a couple of months. Conditions in the refugee camp were heartrending. There was little privacy, feces were everywhere, and clean water was hard to find. At the beginning of 1991 we relocated in Freetown, the capital city. My parents taught in a secondary school in order to sustain our family. I attended that institution for a year. Mingling with students of a different background and orientation was a wonderful experience for me. The academic environment compelled me to remain studious.

The gruesome murder of my two eldest siblings distressed my mom. She suffered persistent illness in Sierra Leone. In fact, she resolved to never return to Liberia until the entire war ended.

In 1991 a civil insurrection broke out in Sierra Leone. To date, it is alleged that Charles Taylor, then the president of Liberia, supported the rebellion, and it is also believed that many Liberians participated actively in the war. In view of this, Liberians in Sierra Leone were under constant surveillance—in some quarters humiliated and ill-treated. We became frightened.

Except for my mom, the rest of my family returned to Liberia in early 1992. By then, Monrovia was experiencing a high semblance of peace and tranquility. The city was secured by thousands of West African peacekeepers. Conditions had improved in that city after the fighting of 1990.

My father lost his job after the cessation of hostilities in Monrovia. Life became again quite unbearable for us. On October 15, 1992, another upsurge of violence broke out in the capital city. My family fled to the suburbs to seek refuge. The fighting lasted for more than two months. Unfortunately, our home got burned in the process. This sad situation greatly distressed my father, as he had expended most of his resources from previous work to construct that house.

Interestingly, amid these difficult circumstances, I was not perturbed. I kept sight of my focus and remained resolute in my pursuit to obtain an education because of my firmly-held belief that it is the best path to success. Essentially, it would provide me the full capacity to contribute meaningfully to my society. I fortunately obtained an academic scholarship in 1993 and maintained the scholarship until my graduation from the University of Liberia in academic year 2001/2002. Accounting and economics were my majors. By dint of my courage, unswerving determination, and diligent application to studies, I won credits and distinctions and graduated with honors, (magna cum laude).

My academic sojourn at UL was painstaking. On countless number of occasions I had barely any food to eat. I studied many days on a hungry stomach. Due to limitation of textbooks and other research materials, we were compelled to make photocopies of the available books. Because of extremely limited income I had to study with friends, most of the time spending the night with them in order to have sufficient time to read. I offered tutorial classes on campus in order to earn some amount of income. By and large my academic sojourn was most difficult.

Isaiah paused a bit in his story as we watched "Kitty" vault off the table to chase a mouse-sized cockroach scurrying across the kitchen floor. We laughed together. He then continued:

Monrovia experienced another outbreak of fighting in 1996. The "Infamous April 6," as it is known, claimed thousands of lives. My father was caught in a cross fire during the fighting. Fortunately, he survived. Again we were forced to flee our home. We sought refuge on the outskirts of Monrovia. Conditions in the area were quite deplorable. A few weeks later, my father became seriously ill. On July 6, 1996, he departed this world. May his soul rest in peace.

The news of the death of my father further troubled my ailing mom. She returned to Monrovia on July 9, 1996. The funeral and burial took place two weeks later.

After the fighting subsided and relative calm was restored to Monrovia, my family resettled around the diplomatic enclave of Mamba Point. We began a new life. My mom found a job at the United States Embassy. After two years of contractual services, she suffered severe illnesses that rendered her physically incapacitated, thus bringing her contract to a virtual end.

By then I was at the University of Liberia. Prior to my graduation in academic 2001/2002, I was recommended to an auditing firm by the chairman of the accounting department. I worked in this institution until my graduation. I was offered several jobs after my graduation. Considering the strenuous economic conditions my family faced, I selected the best option. I worked at that reputable institution up to the latest rounds of war in 2003. My employers fled the country. In September 2003 I was offered another job, as finance officer at the Liberia Baptist Missionary Educational Conventions. In 2004 I was contacted by Northwest Medical Teams International to serve in the capacity of an accountant. I am having

> a wonderful experience, but my primordial objective at the moment is to pursue master's studies toward an MBA degree. Please pray that my dreams and aspirations become reality.
>
> The period between 1990 and 2003 was the most turbulent and destructive time of our nation's history. Hundreds of thousands of people lost their lives, and many millions of dollars of properties were destroyed. Our illiteracy rate is about 85 percent and these people are easily swayed. Until my people are educated, Liberia runs the risks of further degradation and violence. Education along with servant leadership is the sine qua non for lasting peace and development. I desperately want to be part of this new Liberia.
>
> Currently, I live at home with my ailing mother and siblings. Though we are faced with some financial constraints, we are living happily as Christians. We remain forever grateful to the Almighty Lord for His wonderful blessings.

As we finished our time together, "Kitty" leaped back on the table, purring while rubbing against our hands and arms.

A few nights later I faintly heard a few plaintive mews as I lay on my mosquito-netting-covered bed. I got up and searched for kitty but couldn't find her. The next day she was found unmoving in the tall grass behind our tiny house—apparently kicked or clubbed to death by a passing stranger.

After returning home to Oregon, I received this note from my Liberian friend, Isaiah:

> Good Day, Dr. Ken and Mrs. Jo Magee,
>
> It is disheartening to witness another upsurge of hostilities and barbarism that have the proclivity to stall the emerging peace in Liberia.

Elements of an ethnic group, the Mandingoes, clashed with a group made up of several other tribes. Many churches, mosques, schools, other structures, and properties including vehicles were set ablaze. Curfew is now imposed in Liberia. It starts at 4:00 p.m. and goes until 7:00 a.m.

Again, I stand to be corrected. The crux of the matter is that most Liberians are not enlightened.

Ignorance and poverty have plagued our society, and the educated leaders manipulate the illiterates to perpetrate acts intended to satisfy their selfish aggrandizement. This is incredibly frustrating. My deepest apprehension is that Liberia may experience another fierce violence if our leaders do nothing to resolve the deepening conflict—a continuous struggle for economic, political, and religious dominance. Both groups treat each other with disdain. Liberia is founded on Christian principles, and I strongly believe that Liberians should practice tolerance as enshrined in the organic law of the nation. The repercussions of warfare are adverse and far reaching. Most Liberians are not pensive.

I feel despondent and dejected over the behaviors of Liberians. Oh, Lord, please keep our state from further ruin.

Your friend, Isaiah

Is there any hope for Liberia? This story is not yet finished. Aug 20, 2011—Isaiah continued to work for an international organization. He does see progress in his country and now sounds more positive about the future. There is hope.

JOHN MOHAMMED NAYAB

A *good* Afghan friend, John Mohammed Nayab, lies dead. Shot. I just heard it today, November 27, 2004.

Life to him seemed a joy, a celebration of new freedom—shown in his flamboyant dances, his vigorous exercise, impassioned speeches, laughing smile, and deeply caring help. He pointed to the kites flying over Mazar-e-Sharif. This would not have been allowed by the Taliban a few weeks before. He exuded thanksgiving and hope.

During my two months in Afghanistan, John became my favorite driver. Unlike most, he didn't drive like a man dodging machine-gun fire. He carefully slowed or even stopped to allow the disorganized crossing of rickety vehicles, turbaned men, or women in burqas, as well as sheep, donkeys, and camels.

John Mohammed loved to run, and sometimes our managing nurse ran with him while I and others walked on the airport runway near Mazar. We had to carefully stay on this mile-long much-repaired strip of pavement. Twisted remnants of destroyed MiG fighter planes faced one sector, and signs warned of unexploded mines hiding in the grass and bushes that lined other areas.

John lived in a small village. His eyes glistened when he spoke of his wife and their two small children. Several times our nurses were invited to visit his home. (It would have been inappropriate for us menfolk to visit the wife.) The nurses reported that his wife was one of the most beautiful women they had ever seen.

John Mohammed made unforgettable speeches. Once, with loud voice and dramatic movements of hands and arms, he proclaimed at length his hope that the Afghan people would learn to fight with words and not guns. Before we left, John Mohammed Nayab honored Dr. Tom and me with a splendid speech in his native Dari tongue. Our translator relayed magnificent phrases, such as, "You, like the sun, have brought glorious light and warmth to our country."

Near the end of my second trip to Afghanistan, war broke out between competing generals of the Northern Alliance. It drew near. Rumors multiplied. Tanks rumbled through the streets. Tightening restrictions prevented our visiting clinics in nearby villages. John told me, "If the fighting gets too close, you can always come to my house." He would have kept his word.

John Mohammed Nayab, I will always remember your kindness and your laugh. When I called you by your full name, your little black moustache turned up at its ends, your eyes sparkled, and your smile captured us all.

I pray for your family. Afghanistan has lost much. Heaven has gained.

THE SUMATRAN-ANDAMAN EARTHQUAKE AND TSUNAMI

This Indian Ocean earthquake struck on December 26, 2004, with an epicenter off the northwest coast of Sumatra, Indonesia. It was an approximately 9.3 quake caused by megathrust events in land plate subduction zones. The only two larger earthquakes recorded since 1900 are the Chilean earthquake of 1960 and the 1964 quake in Prince William Sound, Alaska. A huge tsunami was generated, killing approximately three hundred thousand people in Indonesia (mainly in Aceh, pronounced 'Ah chey'), and also Sri Lanka, India, Thailand, the Maldives Islands, and Somalia in East Africa. Many aftershocks continued for several months. A separate nearby 8.7 quake occurred close to the Sumatran island of Nias in March of 2005, killing about thirteen hundred.

The plight of affected people generated more than $14 billion in humanitarian aid from many parts of the world. Medical Teams International entered through the hard-hit city of Banda Aceh, and concentrated a major part of its help near Lamno, on Sumatra's northwest coast.

Recent and ongoing fighting between the Free Aceh Movement and the Indonesian military has complicated humanitarian efforts in and around Lamno. The United Nations rated it as a "high risk" security zone. Additionally, Al Qaeda had made nonspecific threats targeting "Western humanitarian workers." Only those directly concerned with emergency efforts or security matters were advised to enter that area.

WHEN THE EARTH MOVED

Our earmuffs softened the sound of the UN helicopter's throbbing blades as I, along with other medical workers, pressed our faces close to the small windows trying to capture the scenes below. With a 9.3 earthquake occurring off the coast of northwest Sumatra on the morning of December 26, 2004, the following Tsunami left pure devastation. The shoreline appeared barren except for torn stumps of trees, twisted ground, and concrete remnants of scattered houses. Here and there we saw a demolished coastal highway, mostly washed away. The beaches and adjacent fields in this area had dropped over two feet. Jungle-draped mountains rose steeply to the east.

The chopper flew toward the town of Lamno, which was built on higher ground and was largely spared. This was not the case with nearby villages at lower elevations. Death had taken most of the area's Sumatran medical workers along with thousands of others. Equipment was stacked behind us–reinforcements for our one permanent clinic, the Static Clinic, and a movable clinic for serving several outlying areas.

A small concrete-block house, fronted by a blue tarp covering an outside waiting area filled with wooden benches, served as our permanent clinic in Lamno. Three rooms inside had small hanging curtains to give some separation and privacy. A wooden chair and tiny table sat in each. A cot also occupied one. Humidity and heat helped me appreciate my loose green scrubs as I and a translator journeyed among those cubicles. I quickly found all of my patients had gripping stories.

Fatima told this story when she brought a tiny crying girl to the clinic: "I crowded into a neighbor's car. It was already full of people. There was only the slightest room on a friend's lap. Hurrying the car toward higher ground, we passed many people who pulled at the locked doors, screaming to get in. But there was no more room, and the furious sea was rapidly gaining. A window near me could not be completely closed. As I worked to raise it, a terrified mother pushed this screaming little bundle through the opening. She fell into my arms. I will care for her. She is loved." Aisyah also brought a small child to me with cough and fever. The child's mother had died in the tsunami, but the infant had been saved. My stethoscope searched the child's chest. The quest revealed one small area of lung congestion, but with each rapid beat of her little heart, I also heard a loud, very abnormal murmur. With a heavy spirit I told this child's savior, Aisyah, as best I could that we would treat the immediate congestion, but much more might be needed that was not available in this part of Sumatra. (The outlook could be poor. Was this child saved only to face a difficult future? Nevertheless, she was loved.)

I tended to Idris, about fifteen years old, because of a painful swollen area of her right thigh. It had been injured as she fled the tsunami. She told me, "I ran with my mother to a nearby hill. When I fell, she helped me up. The water was then receding; my mother turned back to find my sister. She had been at a neighbor's house. But other greater waves came soon. I have not seen either of them since."

Pahmi, also a teenager, ran toward a mosque when he heard the distant roar and cries of great distress. "I saw the stairway to its roof already crowded and ran on." A day later, returning, he found the mosque yet standing and learned that most of those on the stairway had died. Many were his friends.

Pahmi felt exhausted. Thoughts bothered him continuously, and terrible dreams often awakened him at night.

These and many similar stories still tug at my heart.

One month after my arrival, a large UN helicopter was scheduled to pick me up for the first leg of the long trip back to America. My fellow workers at the clinics run by Medical Teams International had graciously given me a free morning prior to my trip home. I asked Muhadi, our excellent driver, if he would take me to the place where his home had been and while there recount the event as he had experienced it. He agreed to tell his story.

Muhadi stood near the center of a large concrete pad that, three months previously, had held his house in the village of Mjung Malhol. While telling of the tragedy, his brow furrowed, and his nearly closed eyes became moist.

> At about ten that morning I heard a deep rumbling, and our house began to shake violently. I hurried outside with my wife and two children. We staggered trying to stand on our feet. Neighbors cried out, and some screamed when part of a nearby house collapsed. Bushes and palm trees shook and swayed. It seemed to be several minutes before the quake lessened and then let up. I have experienced many earthquakes before, but never one of this severity.

> As we stood there not knowing what to do next, we became aware of a distant roar. My wife heard it first. Looking toward the shoreline, we saw the sea raging against the palms and houses nearly a mile away. Bits of buildings and trees were being thrown into the air. I shouted to my wife and children, 'Run and don't look back!"

Motioning toward a nearby ridge, now barren of brush and most trees about halfway up, he continued,

> We ran to that hillside and managed to get near its top with the water clawing close behind. The water churned with parts of houses, trees, and terrified screaming and crying people. Several struggled out, including a man with his wife, our next-door neighbors. They sobbed terribly and could scarcely speak. Their two children had been swept from their arms.
>
> As the wave receded I could see our house still standing with part of the roof torn away. We saw desperate people scattered about in the water, some holding onto debris and others clinging to trees and buildings. Several had reached the roofs of their homes. A bit later an even greater wave met the receding water and pushed it rapidly toward our ridge. My family and others moved to the crest of the hill. I shouted at my neighbors to move. They would have just stood there. Few crawled out of that cauldron. As this wave receded we could see little remaining of our home.
>
> About five minutes later a third and even larger wave surged inland, crashing finally on our hillside. Some spilled across a lower place in the ridge nearby. I thought, *This is our last moment, our saying of good-*

> *byes*, and my wife and children stood with arms wrapped around each other.

Muhadi related,

> This last wave demolished everything to a height of about thirty feet. It left behind a tangle of trees, boards, smashed cars, and human bodies. We were overcome with anguish. The village of Mjung Malhol had been totally swept away. We realized it was a tsunami, caused by the earthquake.
>
> We tried to help other people. Some had broken limbs. Many had large cuts. We felt weak and helpless. After remaining on the hill for nearly eight hours we followed the ridge to higher ground in the town of Lamno. My brother's family lives there, and they remained safe.
>
> The next day I returned to my village—now totally destroyed. I helped others evacuate bodies. These were my friends. It was a tragic time. Of my village's nearly fourteen hundred people, almost a thousand had died.
>
> I later learned that my mother, sister, brother-in-law, and their children all died in the nearby town of Babadua."

Looking about, Muhadi and I saw pieces of clothing, shoes, boards, and broken household furniture still littering the otherwise vacant sand and broken coral flats. Here and there grass was starting to grow. Short shrubs nudged their leaves upward. A single cluster of small white flowers spread their petals beside the concrete slab.

We walked together across the flat and up the hillside, the exact route his family fled. It was steep. My feet slipped in the sand. Trees and brush had been mostly washed away to the height the waves had reached. In places, much of the hillside itself had been swept away.

Standing beside Muhadi on top of the ridge I asked, "Are you going to rebuild your home?" His answer—"I'm so sad. I don't want to live here anymore."

CLOSER THAN RINGSIDE

There have been years of fighting in Aceh Province of northern Sumatra between the Indonesian Army (TNI) and rebel forces (GAM) that sought independence for that region. Leaders in the province wanted the Muslim sharia law to be enforced and complained bitterly of the Indonesian government exploiting the natural resources of Aceh "without appropriate compensation." Because of this we experienced curfews and areas where we could not venture. Armed with automatic weapons, Indonesian military personnel in their dark-green camo uniforms, and always in twos or threes, patrolled the tiny streets of the village of Lamno. While there I heard of only one nearby shooting skirmish—it occurred on the other side of a large muddy river, in an area restricted to our entry. If I knew where the soldiers patrolled, I generally tried to avoid them. In spite of these tensions added to the huge quake and tsunami disaster, pleasant times were common. Generally, the villagers received us with kind smiles and hand waves.

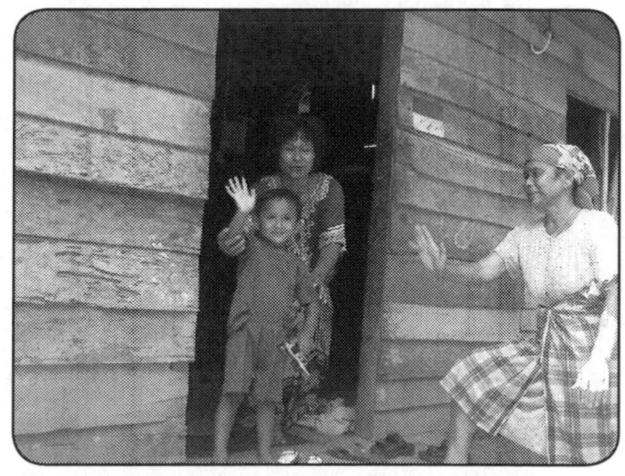

Narrow back alleys, as a rule, proved interesting on our walks to the Static Clinic. With most houses on stilts, the occupants often gathered in these cooler spaces below their homes. We became acquainted with numerous friendly faces, learned the proper local greeting, and waved with our right hands as their culture dictated. Children and even older people waved back. One little tyke tried waving with his left hand and was quickly corrected by his mother, who held down his left hand and raised his right. These routes also took us by small shops with delicious-smelling baked goods, homemade clothes, motor bike repairs, and a most odiferous fish market. Enjoying free range along the way, goats, chickens, ducks, and a tiny breed of turkey foraged along the paths. Where the streets met the nearby jungle, busy monkeys swung from tree to tree and begged for food. Occasionally we heard the calls of a mother tiger from that jungle. Her cub had recently been shot while feeding on a goat.

Have you ever sipped Sumatran coffee? Typically while we watched the cook, the beans were ground, then, with added water, boiled in a small pot. This was poured through a metal strainer into another container. It has a reputation as "the best." We agreed. On our way back from the day's clinic we would sometimes stop to sit around a long table in one of the village's two tiny open-air coffee shops. We'd enjoy this refreshment and time to discuss the day.

Sometimes we would also ask and tell each other about our homes and families and at other times puzzle over our philosophical thoughts. We wondered, "Why would a good God allow thousands of innocent children to die in such a terrible disaster?"

Of our six comely translators, four Muslim girls had been busy learning English in a school in Banda Aceh when the earthquake and tsunami struck. Many of their classmates died. Two lost family members. They knew grief. They all loved Aaron, a young American nurse working with us, who especially gifted us by adding humor to these times together. Sobering subjects such as what to do about Abdulla's huge facial tumor were often replaced with Aaron's raucous laughter.

One evening as eight of us sat around a long table sipping variations of the delicious coffee, one of our group asked our Sumatran translators, "What have you learned from the tsunami?"

There was silence for a bit, except for a distant rumble of thunder from towering cumulus clouds above nearby jungle-draped mountains. Then I wrote down their thoughtful answers:

"Patience."

"We have to unite ourselves together all over the world."

"Brotherhood is very important. It is everything."

"Pay more attention to other people and feel how they feel."

"We must learn about the earthquake and tsunami."

"Great adventure."

"We can integrate our faith."

While talking, I became aware of an ominous figure beside a nearby table. Several times before, I had seen him standing in the middle of Lamno's primary intersection, where its only main street joined the disrupted Sumatran coastal highway. Motorbikes, cars, and an occasional truck would whiz close by. He didn't seem to care. A lightweight coat covered most of his body. It was black with a white waistband. He seemed to be watching us closely.

Our six excellent lady translators were sitting with me at the end of the table closest to this strange-acting fellow. I noted him edging slowly toward us and actually took his picture. Unlike my usual approach, I did not ask for permission. He stood there mute, then slowly slipped right up to the end of our table. The young ladies, of course, were also very aware of his presence. Increasing strain was obvious in their voices and actions. They shifted about in their chairs and even looked ready to run. Nana scooted her chair back a bit and rolled her eyes. Masna's lips tightened, and her brow furrowed. Rahmi gave an almost inaudible squeal and started to stand up.

The visitor seemed propelled by their show of discomfort. Lowering his head he dashed quickly down the underside of the entire length of the table. This produced more squeals and vacated chairs in total disarray. His horns scraped the table as he made this quick run. Emerging, he let out a loud goaty "baaa" and scampered into the nearby field. I think he was laughing. We all joined him in the hilarity. It was therapeutic.

Only one day before at this same table, four fighting cocks had moved their squawking tussle from that same field to a more interesting site among our legs. Certainly it was exciting! Closer than ringside.

ABDULLA

Our busy day at the Static Clinic in Lamno seemed almost over when a thin man with a terribly bulged deformity of his right face appeared. He stood quietly under the edge of the blue tarp stretched above the wooden benches of our clinic's outside waiting area. His small sister stood with him. They both looked dispirited. The scene's background included a tiny house across a narrow dirt road, positioned in front of the brownish water of a large snake-infested pond with crowding jungle on the far side. Curious, I crossed the small benched area with my coworker, Dr. Mary, and an interpreter.

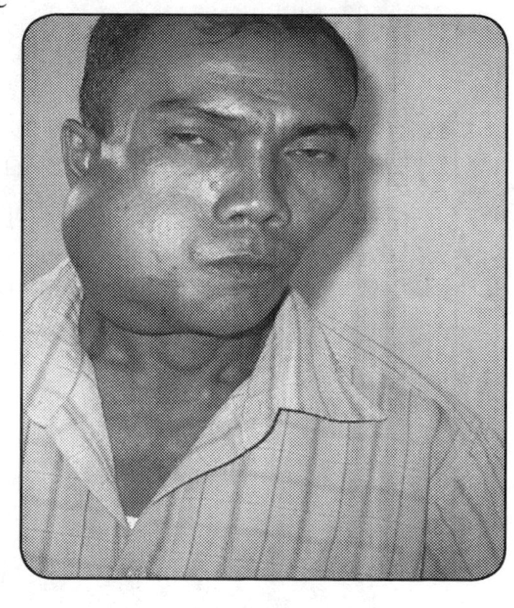

Our interpreter informed us, "His name is Abdulla."

Abdulla then related this story: "With the pulling of a tooth three years ago, I noticed the starting of swelling. It has grown much since then. Today I went to the puskesmas (hospital) in Lamno and in previous months I have visited other clinics in northern Sumatra.

No one has given me any hope. It is very difficult to eat. Often people are afraid of me. Even my children sometimes avoid me."

Deep feelings touched our hearts, and we arranged for him to be seen the next day.

Abdulla returned with his wife in the morning. He seemed sad but stoic. She seemed desperate. We found he lived and farmed near a small village several kilometers beyond Lamno. They had the responsibility for three children—ages five, eleven, and fourteen years.

I carefully felt the large mass that protruded from the right side of his face. It felt very firm, not movable, and it surprised me that gentle manipulation elicited no tender response. No enlarged lymph nodes could be felt below in his neck or above the collarbone. Examination inside his mouth revealed a large ulcerated sore in the right mandibular area. No teeth remained in that jaw area. The left side looked and moved normally. Further exam revealed healthy heart, lungs, and abdomen, without evidence of disease in the remainder of his body.

We speculated as to the type of the tumor. The slow growth over three years without evidence of spread to other areas made it likely to be a noncancerous, although aggressive, tumor. Our good dentist, Terry, thought it was probably bony in origin. It realistically might soon cause a terrible death by the obstruction of his eating or his breathing, or by erosion into an artery, with a subsequent massive bleed.

Hope? The tiny local hospital had no x-ray equipment. We knew of no surgeon available in that part of Sumatra who was surgically able to undertake such a complicated procedure. Another nearby medical NGO (nongovernment organization) had no suggestions. Tragedy appeared not far away for this family in an already tsunami-stricken area.

We began a prayerful search with a phone call to our headquarters in Banda Aceh, Sumatra. We also contacted the home office of MTI (Medical Teams International) about the possibility of sending Abdulla to Singapore, should no other option present itself. Our coworker Teresa, RN, e-mailed a friend on Mercy Ship, the name of an organization that had several hospital ships. One of these waited and worked near the recently quake-stricken islands off the west coast of Sumatra.

I saw Abdulla three more times while we waited and hoped for some positive answer. Teresa's friend e-mailed back that a group of physicians in Banda Aceh would be able to see him, and possibly could recommend transfer to Mercy Ship. Other thoughts were put on hold, and our good logistician, Kirk, offered to go with Abdulla to Banda Aceh. Kirk was determined to find help. He later wrote, "I didn't give much thought to things not working out. I was a little naïve."

Dr. Leo, a Houston internist with MTI, in addition to the press of his clinical work, consented to take over the large load of logistics at Lamno during Kirk's absence.

Abdulla smiled with a lopsided grin when told of the hope in Banda Aceh. He seemed much relieved. His wife and sister practically danced. They seemed a bit disappointed because Abdulla's wife would not be able to go on the helicopter with him.

In Banda Aceh answers again proved very complicated. The physicians there felt the tumor seemed beyond surgical help, with one exception, an Australian, Dr. Bill. He believed the possibility of a life-saving operation existed. He and Kirk continued to look for a positive answer, in spite of other doctors' great apprehension, not advising transfer to Mercy Ship or offering alternative suggestions.

Just before he left Sumatra, Dr. Bill went to a small temporary field hospital that the International Committee of the Red Cross out of Switzerland had set up close behind a soccer field near Banda Aceh. Here he spoke with a Hungarian surgeon, Dr. Kazmer, who agreed the surgery actually seemed possible. After some persuasion of others, it was decided to let Dr. Kazmer try. He felt it could be accomplished by resecting (cutting out) the small remnant of right jawbone along with the huge tumor. Reconstruction of the bone wouldn't be possible.

Meanwhile, Abdulla's wife and five-year-old daughter came by bus to join him.

Kirk e-mailed me, "The little girl is as cute as a button and reminds me of my own daughter at home. I bought her a dress and pants suit and some stuffed animals and visited them every day in the hospital, as long as I could remain in Banda Aceh. I tried to financially help them out as a family, but still feel as though it wasn't enough."

Later, Dr. Kazmer wrote Kirk, who forwarded the e-mail note to me—now home in America: "In regard to your patient, Mr. Abdulla, I can tell you only good news. He was operated on two weeks ago, and even if the procedure was not easy at all, it went well. We did a tracheotomy, (neck opening into the airway), as the first step, and then the benign tumor was removed. Clinically it looked like osteoid osteoma. The complete right side of the mandible, (right jawbone), was removed. The tumor had entered the right tempero-mandibular joint, (where the jawbone joins the skull), so I had to remove the destroyed joint as well. This means even in a developed country this patient would not have had any chance for reconstruction. So I think we made the right decision to do it here as soon as possible. Also, we were able to close the oral mucosa, (lining on the inside of the mouth), which made me happy and made it an easier procedure for the patient.

"The post-op period passed without any complication. At the beginning we had to feed him through a nasogastric tube. A few days after the surgery we removed the tracheostomy tube, and the opening closed by itself. After one week he began to drink and eat soft food. Later he learned to keep the left side of his jaw in good position so the remainder of the mandibula had good occlusion. He could chew. The wound healed nicely, and we discharged him two days ago.

"Our surgical team was happy. His family was joyous. They left for home on a bus. Thank you and others for the part you took in this success."

(I can easily picture Abdulla and his little daughter giving each other hugs.)

Dr. Kazmer also reported, "Only a few hours after Abdulla's discharge, a hurricane struck northern Sumatra and totally destroyed the temporary Red Cross hospital."

SRI LANKA

Sri Lanka is an island country off the southeast coast of India that has been known by many names. While the English dominated the area, it was called Ceylon. In 1947 it was granted independence, and in 1972 its name was changed to Sri Lanka, meaning "resplendent land" in Sanskrit. Nicknames for the island have included the "Isle of Teaching," "India's Teardrop," and "Pearl of the Indian Ocean."

The inhabitants are now 74 percent Sinhalese, descendants of Buddhists who migrated from northern India long ago. In the twelfth century AD, the Tamils, mostly Hindus, migrated from southern India and eventually established their domain in northern Sri Lanka. They, along with a small number of Christians, account for about 18 percent of the population. About 7 percent of the present inhabitants are Islamic descendants of the Moors. The total population now numbers about twenty million, and the present literacy rate is 90 percent.

The Portuguese came in 1505. They were later driven out by the Dutch, who ceded the island to the English in 1802. In the mid-1980s, severe hostilities broke out between the government and armed Tamil separatists. They fought for an independent country in the island's northern and eastern areas. Hundreds of Tamils fled back to southern India and the West.

The Indian Ocean earthquake and subsequent tsunami of December 26, 2004, smashed into this already ravaged island. Sri

Lanka's east coast lost thousands of people and many camps for internally displaced people formed. Warfare continued. Medical Teams International and many others sent help to this devastated land.

SRI LANKA, A TALE OF TWO COUNTRIES

It was about 1:00 a.m. when we arrived at the Northwest Medical Teams headquarters in Colombo. It had been a long trip from home in Klamath Falls, Oregon, through Portland to Vancouver, British Columbia, and on to Hong Kong, Bangkok, and finally to Sri Lanka's capitol city. I was pleased to meet and exchange hugs with some friends I'd journeyed and labored with in the past. But my sitter was worn out. I looked forward to sleep.

There, in the wee morning hours, our in-country medical director, Carol, RN, informed us that we'd be leaving for the other side of this huge island country in about five hours. We would be traveling in two vehicles for about 150 miles, and then separate to go to our specific areas of work. NWMTI was just opening a new area of refugee clinics on the far northeastern coast of Sri Lanka. I had anticipated I'd be sent to Kalmunai, much farther south on the same tsunami-devastated coast. She would tell us more as we traveled. In spite of my anticipatory adrenaline and the moisture-laden heat, I slept well.

Others in our group included Dr. Leo, a kind friend from the past (an internist from Houston, Texas); Dr. Wendy, an internist from Cambridge, Massachusetts; Dr. Oren, an internist from Denver, Colorado; Jenna, a pediatric nurse from Portland, Oregon; and Norma, a psychiatric nurse from Vancouver, British Columbia. Sri Lankan staff would be traveling with us.

As we loaded our many bags into the waiting van and ambulance, I glanced around. The nearby houses would complement any city. Across the narrow pavement in front of our headquarters was a green band of tropical bushes and trees from which issued calls of birds new to my ears. Just beyond meandered a murky river, broad and dimpled here and there by unknown occupants. My curiosity was piqued. (I later, on return to Colombo, observed that there were not only fish but large monitor lizards, up to five and six feet in length.) Nearby a very modern apartment building rose forty floors.

Traveling eastward I found Colombo, Sri Lanka's largest city, stretching for miles. Even this early in the morning its paved streets were crowded with people, three-wheeled tuk-tuks, autos, and numerous motorbikes. Here and there cows and goats intermingled with the traffic. About an hour and a half later we drove eastward along a well-marked, winding, two-lane road. There were many small villages lining the highway, which left very little space for the crowding jungle to touch its edge. Businesses selling clothes or cycles were separated by shops with large suspended clumps of yellow to green bananas, and piles of mangos, papaya, and coconuts. We began to see hills rising out of the dense jungle. A few hours later our driver pulled into a small restaurant with a wide front porch. While eating lunch we talked about our assignments. Carol wanted me to go northward with Wendy and Oren to help in starting the new work north of Trincomalee in the Kuchchaveli area. Inwardly my adrenalin level rose. It would be grand being involved in a new area where thousands of refugees received very limited medical care. However, I knew that historically it is in the middle of the area where warfare between the Tamil and Sinhalese factions had been intense. We would be isolated and without phone, radio, or Internet contact.

Soon afterward the highway separated, and Leo, Jenna, and Norma headed southward toward Kalmunai, along with our driver, while Carol, Oren, Wendy, and I turned northward toward Trincomalee in the ambulance. I felt sad to leave my good friend Leo.

Descending from the high hills of central Sri Lanka, we wound our way gradually past valleys filled with rice paddies. Cattle of Brahman heritage and water buffalo were common. Jungles and some more open grasslands edged our now-broken roads. Villages were few, but military posts with watching Sinhalese soldiers surrounded by barriers of green sandbags became common. The unmarked pavement had broken edges, was lacking in places, and everywhere had a rippled jolting surface. Once we stopped to watch and tip a roadside entrepreneur who showed us woven baskets holding two cobras, one erect, in striking mode, and a leashed monkey with bright-colored trousers. A troupe of wild elephants brought us to another stop. We were cautioned to keep at a distance. Cameras clicked as elephant trunks sprayed their backs with dirt and pulled at leaves. Nearby wild peacocks strutted bright blue necks with fanned tails.

DIARY

11-7-05 p.m. What an interesting and scenic drive we had from Colombo today. Thank you, Lord, for the privilege of walking with You. Thank You for your care. Strengthen my memory.

11-8-05. A restful night near Trincomale. The room had lots of interesting bugs. Nearby I hear the sound of the Indian Ocean. Trinco has the best harbor on the East coast of Sri Lanka. Both factions would like to control it. I count sixty-one boats out on the water, each with two or three people. They appear to be throwing out nets and drawing them in. Most are motorized. One nearby has an outrigger. I hear the caws of crows—black with gray heads. Walking outside for a better view, there is a thump beside me—a large coconut. Better move out from under those palms.

The sand is piled high just ahead—question if long-term or related to the Tsunami waves? A dog lies on this ridge—brown and black, short hair, skinny with pointed muzzle. As I approach he trots away toward a row of beached boats.

A good breakfast—Almost American in type with scrambled eggs containing tiny bits of tomato, homemade bread—toasted, with butter and jam.

We had to wait 'til shops opened. Visited a pharmacy, where we presented a list of meds needed. We arranged to return later in the day to pick them up. They don't have several and quantity will be insufficient with some. We will have to search for more meds back in Colombo at a future time.

Picked up Lars, a German physician who we met at breakfast. He has worked here for about eight months. He states his primary purpose is helping with EMT (emergency medical tech) training. He did emergency work in Deutschland. Didn't seem to have an organization with which he is collaborating. I wondered. He traveled with us to his temporary residence near a Sisters of Charity clinic just north of Trincomale.

After getting meds (very limited but what is available), we picked up T. Posamfokij, the village coordinator, and headed for "home," Kuchchavelli. Traveling north from Trincomalee, our ambulance bumped and wove along the coastline. Pavement and gravel soon became nonexistent. We maneuvered around and drove through holes, often deep with sandy water. Eastward spread iridescent greens and blues of the Indian Ocean with white breakers on beaches of yellow sand. Westward, jungle pushed into the road's edge. Small bushes, some flowered with lavender or gold, interwoven vines, and a variety of trees of all sizes composed scarcely penetrable jungle. This beauty contrasted with miles of broken remnants of boats and houses and barren trees—residue of the tsunami. Amid this, red, yellow, and purple flowers and new jungle growth were pushing up, trying to hide the terror of those waves. We saw frequent large refugee camps with rows of small houses made of wood, mud, and corrugated metal, commonly thatched above with branches of palms. It had been raining for four days but had mostly stopped. Immense brown ponds of water were evident among the houses. Several men with muddy legs and clinging, wet clothes were working to deepen drainage ditches. An occasional child or adult hurrying between buildings paused to watch us pass. From the back of the ambulance my neck turned and eyes searched, trying to miss nothing. As the ambulance twisted and lurched, my stomach began to do the same.

We saw many patrols of government soldiers, looking for mines, searching the sides of the road with long-handled rakes, or waiting in their small fortresses of green sandbags. Occasionally they stopped us briefly to look and question, then waved us on. More and more commonly we saw cement walls, blackened by the fires of war, where once had stood lovely homes. Many roadside areas were bordered by tiny red poles or marked by small red on white signs bearing a skull and crossbones with a warning—"Land Mines." A large deer hobbled slowly away from one area of dense brush, dangling a back leg, and a front leg bare of hair and skin below its knee. Our driver commented, "Land mine." Sadness ran deep. It seemed a remote country, totally different from Colombo—a mixture of both great beauty and tragedy.

Our house in Kuchchavelli had been hit hard by the Tsunami and is yet being repaired. Paint smells fresh, but there is unsafe water and limited kitchen facilities. Much needs doing, but we will get by. A small, largely destroyed hospital sits nearby. Part is being rebuilt, and a Sri Lankan, Dr. Eranza, now runs a busy clinic. His is the only help for some seven thousand people in refugee camps. His wife and child are back in Colombo. This area is too isolated and unsafe to bring them. He promises to tell me more at a later time. I do admire Dr. Eranza.

A river north of Kuchchavelli has a two-car ferry that helps us connect to country still farther north. A 40-horsepower outboard engine is bolted to a tiny platform on one side of the ferry. Its operator sits steering, and two other men detach and attach mooring lines and raise and lower cables across the ends of the boat. It chugs right along, for perhaps two hundred meters, and then swivels and bumps the wooden ramp on the opposite side with certainty. A small bed of red and white flowers has been planted and nurtured beside the landing ramp. Lovely.

The tiny town we encounter is composed of many small homes along narrow, sandy roads full of chuckholes. Corners are abrupt and generally blinded with buildings, necessitating the honking of horns to lessen the possibility of collision. Mostly Muslim folks live here—the women with long dresses and head scarves, the men with tightly clinging white caps.

We visited six or seven internally displaced people (IDP) camps and village sites. Often they are a combination of a partially destroyed village and makeshift mud or metal huts. They are home for a mixture of Tamil and Sinhalese people—mostly Hindu and

Buddhist with occasional groups of Muslims and a scattering of Christians. On the surface they seem to be getting along well ... but there is the reality of years of warfare. I felt uneasy and wondered, *Will this flare again?* I certainly hoped not.

A cobra slithered rapidly across the road ahead and into the nearby brush. It appears about six feet in length—the hinder half of a large, half-swallowed lizard protrudes from its mouth. Wish I'd had time to take a picture.

11-8-05 p.m. Arriving back at Kuchchavelli, we found a frightened young mother with her tiny infant. Dr. Eranza was gone, so Dr. Wendy saw the baby. It was crying, had a fever and some cough but had clear lungs, was not dehydrated, and was still nursing well. She procured some medicine and arranged for the little one to be seen again soon.

This evening we spent much time around our supper table talking, while eating a meal of rice and fish, cooked by Terrance, our houseboy. We later went through and arranged our medical supplies according to what we expected to encounter the following day.

One of the richest parts of these journeys is listening and getting to know each other in depth. I described myself as a person who tried to be a Christ follower, Dr. Wendy described herself as one who tried to follow the Buddha, and Dr. Oren, of Jewish background, said later that he was like the name given for Jacob, "Israel," meaning, "One who wrestles with God." We concluded that that was good.

We also considered the possibility of saying a blessing before each meal and what that would mean. Together we decided it meant telling that for which we were thankful, and what our hopes were for the future, both immediate and distant. Wendy suggested that we take turns saying our blessings at each meal. Oren and I agreed.

11-9-05. The long evening of medicine sorting and talking produced a short night. I slept okay. Made ready to leave for our first camp. Have most but not all the meds we might need. At breakfast Wendy prayed for help for the day.

What a privilege to spend many days visiting clinics full of hurting people.

RESPLENDENT LAND

In spite of the terrible suffering from the years of warfare and the Indian Ocean tsunami of 2004, Sri Lanka is indeed a resplendent land. Twice, because of increased threats of warfare, we evacuated our headquarters briefly, traveling southward and to the interior mountains. This did give us added chances to enjoy the beauties of mountains near Kandy, covered with tea bushes. Groups of ladies dotted those green hillsides picking leaves. We visited drying sheds with long bins deep in leaves, and areas where they further processed leaves.

At one stop a monkey, edging close in a nearby tree, suddenly descended with hand into the pocket of a friend, then rapidly swung high into the same tree with a candy bar in its hand.

From a distance, we enjoyed a herd of elephants, all sizes, using trunks to eat from the jungle and to spray dust over their backs.

Other sights included dung beetles digging holes in the dirt and burying themselves; tortoises with large, colorful shells traveling paths near the ocean beaches; trees full of the brilliance of peacocks; and wild jackals (much like our coyotes) hunting stealthily through more open grasslands.

Sri Lanka, Resplendent Land—the name is deserved. May its turmoil vanish.

OLD JOE

He was one of the most memorable patients I'd had in my many years of private medical practice in Oregon. Old Joe didn't appear very often. This time he said he had "a sore foot." I knew he worked cattle in the open ranges of eastern Oregon in the summers and fed cattle in fenced feedlots near Bonanza in the winters. This consisted of many hours of mud, manure, and wagons distributing bales of grass and alfalfa hay.

His unkempt state and aroma were obvious as he hobbled down the short hallway to an examining room. Old Joe wore a torn broad-brimmed hat, darkened with the sweat and grime of years and its use as a switch while moving cattle. It would have been no surprise to see a few sprigs of grass taking root in its brim. His face, covered with gray stubble, was creased with time and weather.

I motioned him toward a captain's chair in the exam room with, "Joe, it's good to see you. Sit yourself down here."

"Thanks, Doc," he responded as he gingerly settled into the chair, right leg extended, and obviously relieved to be off his feet.

He was about as I remembered him—thin, a little older. His torn blue work shirt had a brownish long john top showing through. His jeans could stand alone in the corner at night. I wondered if he ever gave them that chance. His boots, formerly brown, now drew my attention. You could tell he had been feeding cattle lately and didn't worry about where he stepped.

"How long has your foot been hurting you?"

"Three days, Doc."

"Have you had a horse step on it? Have you had any trouble before—like cramps when you walk, or a sore on it?"

To all these questions and more, Old Joe responded, "No, Doc."

"Let's get this boot off." I motioned toward his extended leg.

"You got to help me, Doc. It ain't been off in a while." I certainly believed that.

"Joe, you need to get a bath once in a while."

"Doc, "he said with a bit of a grin, "the watering tank's been froze over."

Together we struggled with that boot, and it finally gave way. As I next peeled his odiferous sock downward, I was betting on an infected foot or possibly some gangrenous toes. But there, under the arch of his foot, appeared a sizable roll of bills.

The outer one was a twenty. Both Joe and I were relieved.

"I wondered where I'd put my dang money," he chuckled.

We both had a good laugh.

THE LOG

"Your patient, Bill Biaggi, is here and in bad shape," was the phone call I'd received only minutes before. Little did I know that this visit to the emergency room would be different from any other I'd ever experienced. It was late, just before midnight, cold outside, with winter-like weather. Dee, the emergency nurse, motioned me with a hand holding a blackened washrag, toward a curtained cubicle and said, "Bill's in here."

As she pulled the curtain aside, I was met by the strong smell of burnt wood and the sight of a supine figure, black from his cowboy boots to the top of his disheveled hair. Bill was in obvious pain. Beside him stood his good wife, Peggy, with deep concern etched on her face. With only the slightest movement he moaned. A quick exam showed extreme tenderness in his pelvic area, increased by any movement of it or his upper legs. He was covered head to toe with soot, but no obvious burns were found. I ordered x-rays, lab tests, an IV, and pain medicine. As the nurse added some warmed blankets and gently continued the cleaning process, Peggy began to fill me in on the day.

Bill and Peggy's family owned a ranch in Swan Lake Valley. Here follows the story as Peggy, and later Bill and her sister, Pat, told it.

Several heifers had found their way up onto massive Swan Lake Rim, which stretches about ten miles to a mountain with the same name. This unfenced land was owned by the Bureau of Land Management. On a cold day in May they needed to move the heifers back to their own property, where feed hay waited. Peggy had recently delivered a daughter, Toni, and shouldn't yet ride. Pat, her sister, was available to help Bill.

Below the rim a ten-mile-long unimproved road led along the north side of the valley, passable for their four-wheel-drive pickup. Pulling a horse trailer, they bounced and slogged, making their way to where a steep winding road, little more than a trail, headed up the ridge. After unloading the horses, Bill and Pat mounted and, with digging hooves, were carried up toward the rim. Their two eager dogs accompanied them: Frank, a medium-haired, black and tan cattle dog, and Fred, a smaller dog with white on his chest and a brown muzzle. Bill's horse was a "greenbroke" sorrel gelding, three or four years old.

After reaching Styles Bench, a large area about six hundred feet above the valley, they saw cattle tracks all about, imprinted in snow and mud and pointing in many directions. The afternoon was fairly young, and they decided that Pat would look toward the east, and Bill would search westward. Briefly they noted the beauty of the area, partly wooded with rocky bluffs above, but they had work to get done. The dogs, Frank and Fred, trotted along with Bill.

Riding westward, Bill passed a little spring where cattle had obviously been watering. Nearby a small group of uneasy heifers sidled away. Many tracks indicated more to the west. He was in a shallow canyon now. Passing a tiny reservoir filled with water, he pulled his young gelding leftward off the main trail to check a partly hidden slope to the south. It was there that the horse slipped in the snow and mud, became agitated, started bucking, and fell. Bill landed next to a large log with the horse partly on top of him. His pain was immense. The young sorrel scrambled up, turned, and ran back in the direction from which they'd come. Bill lay powerless to stop him. At first the two dogs ran a short distance after the horse, then they turned and came back to Bill.

Lying there in mud and snow in severe pain, Bill realized his terrible predicament. He could not move his hips or legs. Would he be found? Would he die before then? Would he freeze to death? He determined to try to survive. It was painful to search for the lighter in his left front pocket—but he did, and tugged it out along with his pocket knife. Struggling, he dug into the large log and found some rotten, dry, loose wood. From under the edge of the log he added a handful of half-dry pine needles. A tiny fire finally reached upward, and smoke spread outward with a little heat. He tried to get close but movement remained nearly impossible.

Nearby, Frank and Fred watched and frequently whined. They seemed to understand that Bill was in trouble. Frank soon snuggled down close beside Bill, and Fred lay on top of him. The smoky fire burnt on.

Far to the East, Pat had found a few scattered heifers. While gathering them up, the gelding came trotting up with his empty saddle. Obviously something had happened, and Bill might be in trouble. She grasped the sorrel's reins and, leading him, rode back in the direction from which he'd come. Thoughts raced through her mind. *Was Bill hurt? Was he alive? Would she be able to find him?* As she worked her way westward, she expected to find the dogs It was getting later in the day, blustery, and snowing off and on. Through her heavy coat she felt the cold, and it would soon be hard to see. She hoped he'd light a fire, and with the blowing wind she also watched for smoke.

Pat passed through the general area where Bill lay but couldn't see the fire, and no dogs appeared. She then decided to ride off the rim to where the parked pickup waited. After loading the horses in the trailer she drove slowly along the bottom of the ridge watching above for smoke or fire. Light was fading and none appeared. After returning to the start of the very primitive road at the bottom of the hill, she unloaded the horses. Mounting her own horse and leading the gelding, Pat returned to the large bench where she'd last seen Bill. Darkness grew deeper.

While circling back through the area to the west, Frank and Fred heard her, and Fred came bounding down the slope, tail wagging. Pat related, "I really smiled to myself," and she followed the dog back to the log where Bill lay.

Obviously they were happy to see each other, but the predicament needed further solutions. Although Pat had a CB radio, repeated tries could reach no one. She then removed the blankets from the gelding and added them to Bill's protection. The dogs stayed with him as Pat rode back to the truck. Down below, driving a couple of miles south of Styles Bench, she managed to first contact Peggy at home, and then Tom, her husband. Peggy called for an ambulance, but the emergency medical team wasn't able to drive their vehicle the last two miles up to the bench to get the injured rancher. Thankfully a neighbor, Stanley Petersen, who had a four-wheel-drive pickup, put a mattress in the back and took Pat and Tom and the two EMTs (five people in all) up the mountain to bring Bill back to the ambulance.

The two dogs moved aside as the EMTs carefully transferred Bill to a stretcher and then placed him on the mattress in the back of the pickup. Frank and Fred jumped right in there with him. It was crowded, and one of the paramedics wanted to make the dogs follow behind, but Bill told the medics, "I'm not going without my dogs. I wouldn't be here if it wasn't for their sticking by me and giving me warmth." With six people, a mattress, and two dogs, the return was a full pickup load.

Bill later related how he felt every painful bounce, both coming down off the hill and in the ambulance heading ten miles farther before getting to paved road. He has been described by his family as "one who wouldn't back away from anything." Recovery from his broken pelvis and leg was long and difficult, but Bill made it.

Forty years later, on a snowy fall day, I went with Larry Jespersen, a nearby rancher, to try and locate the place where Bill was found. Peggy had described the location to Larry. As we came up onto Styles Bench, the area of the search, its beauty was forceful. Groves of stately yellow-barked Ponderosa pine rose among scattered junipers and areas of mountain mahogany. High above, the snowy slopes were interrupted by huge fields of massive boulders topped by rocky cliffs reaching upward. I enjoyed the strong fragrance of sage and junipers. All of these brought back memories of numerous wintertime adventures following my hound dogs. Walking westward along the trail about a mile, we found a little spring piped into a watering tank, and just beyond that a small dry reservoir. About a hundred yards farther and up the slope to our left was a log covered with snow. It had a depression near its center. A cool breeze touched us as we brushed away the snow. The indentation had been deeply blackened by fire.

JARBIDGE—ANTIDOTE FOR COMPASSION FATIGUE

Here is a letter composed of journaling for my family during and following one of my many retreats into remote "cougar lands."

Dear family, it would be so excellent to have you all here with me—camping at the forks of the Jarbidge River in southern Idaho right beside the Nevada border. It's so different from the hurries and stresses of life while caring night and day for people in my medical office, in the hospital, and in their homes.

Starting at 3:00 p.m. on Saturday, we journeyed 650 miles through the night, stopping to sleep a couple of times, and then slept an hour more while waiting for the store in Rogerson, Idaho, to open Sunday morning. We needed to purchase two gallons of milk and fill my Land Cruiser's tank with gasoline. Glenn drove all the way. I'm glad he likes to drive, but I felt a little guilty not doing some of it.

Wow, you should see the majestic rocky cliffs stretching hundreds of feet above the sides of this bounding river. Patches of sagebrush protrude from spots of snow and cling to a few brief slopes. Scattered junipers add beauty. Our dear friends, Flo and Steve, arrived here ahead of us and already have set up tents. We helped cut some dead juniper remnants from around our camp for firewood. The opened wood shows magnificent artistry—twisted rings with many shades of yellow, dark red, and purple. We feel a bit reluctant to use it for firewood. Close by some flocks of cedar waxwings with their little topknots entertain us along with a flock of robins feeding on juniper berries.

We've already seen several cougar tracks in spots of snow—a female with her two kittens and a single large cat, which printed the night before only a hundred yards from our campsite. The big cat crossed the river and climbed right up a rocky bluff. Steve put his dog, Apache, on it, but up on those steep, dry rocks the trailing scent became extremely slow, so we stopped.

Monday night a brisk wind pushed up the canyon. Steve went out to firm up some of our tent moorings. Patsy, his and Flo's little house dog, scurried out there to help dig up some rocks. In one gust a big kettle fell off the stove, and Patsy ran into the cooking tent and peered down into that large pan as though looking for the cause of the racket. David and Emil (young grandchildren), you would really love Patsy—she keeps track of everything.

Monday we hiked on the East Fork of the Jarbidge—Idaho side—and got more good up-an-down exercise. My skillful hound, Cindy, enjoyed working some aged cougar tracks—nothing fresher than one or two days old. Largely the ground remains bare, so little scent lingered. When you consider that cougars commonly travel long distances, we couldn't follow far. We found one area where a cougar bedded down and invited a deer to join him at mealtime.

Tuesday we traversed the rocks and slopes of another area on the East Fork of the Jarbidge. My dog, Flo, limped with sore feet that night. Without much snow and lots of rocks, we have been trying to figure out some easier path of trekking and have a "bright" idea for Wednesday. The dogs did have a little tail wagging around old deer carcasses, and especially at one hosting magpies, a couple of golden eagles, and ravens finishing up a very recent kill. They sure clean up their plates!

Today (I think it's a Wednesday in February), we hunted part of the day on a much less rocky, sagebrush-clothed ridge. A herd of long-horned cattle searched for clumps of grass in the valley below. Gorgeous sunny weather helped warm us. Saw lots of deer fur and cougar scrapings, (mounds the males make by urinating on a spot, then scraping with their front feet to mark their territory.) Saw tracks of various sizes—one big fellow and other smaller ones, but nothing fresh. I sweat, and ate oranges, drank water, and ate snow in the scattered places where I could find a melting patch. Some of it has a distinct sage flavor, so one has to be a little choosy. At day's end, my pockets were full of sagebrush leaves.

Flo and Steve's little speckled dog, Patsy, thinks she's a people. When Steve goes out to load up the hounds, she follows along acting important, and then snaps her teeth and barks, "Helping the big dogs jump into the dog box."

We continue to enjoy good grub. Flo is a superb camp cook! We've had excellent stew, chicken, and pork roast, and had an elk steak tonight—plus lots of good things to go with these main dishes. Then at night we get to go soak in the hot water at nearby Murphy Hot Springs.

There's a little church group being started by the few people living at Murphy's. It meets on Thursday afternoons—would be fun to go but isn't at a time we can manage.

Thursday was our last day to hunt. Cindy picked up a medium-sized lion track and worked it about a third of a mile, getting out onto dry ground away from the moist hillside. There the scent evaporated. The track appeared about a day old.

We're going to barbecue some beef tonight. I've got some Manzanita wood busily making coals.

I'm mighty thankful for Steve and his wife, Flo. I've hunted for years with Steve. We agreed when we first began hunting together that we wouldn't talk about medicine. That has been very therapeutic for me. And I'm so thankful for my good friend, Glenn, who has accompanied me on several trips. But most of all it is so excellent to have a superb wife to go home to.

Friday, on traveling homeward, we decided to drive a remote desert road across Southern Idaho from Murphy's to Bruneau. Most of the winter it would have been impassable, but the previous week and longer of dry weather made it possible to save two hours of time. It carried us across a military range, and we did climb into some higher country with drifts and had to backtrack a bit, but it ended up being a good shortcut—unlike some I've taken.

By the way, let me tell you of my dream Thursday night. I found I could make a hole in the center of a piece of bread and twirl it on my index finger. I practiced, and shortly I could tilt my finger sideways and twirl it in all directions while skipping around the room—and then I was able to tilt it upside down, and it would yet stay on my finger. I next tried it with both hands. I could do it! Finally with slices of bread on all my fingers, I could twirl all of them at once.

Think I will go on a tour and …

Sunday. It is good being back in my temporary home. Glenn and I had lots of things to talk about on our homeward way. We sighted numerous deer, antelope, wild burros, and other critters. Glenn told me how in recent times the scriptures became very alive for him, and how he's become very hungry to know God better. Such extraordinary experiences are deeply imbedded in my memory.

Not many years later Glenn passed away with heart problems. I wrote this note for his memorial service:

> Dear Glenn,
>
> You've beat me in getting there, but I'll join you one of these times not far off. I'm expecting our Leader to appoint you to give me a long tour. One of the reasons I chose YOU is because you are prone to dawdle, pausing to look at the tracks and flowers like I do. I love that.
>
> Let's stand on the edge of a canyon again, just like we did at Jarbidge, and feel the warm afternoon sun and feel the cool breeze. Why don't you bring along a couple of your dogs, and I will bring along Ginger and Red. Maybe an old cougar will wander by, and we can play "chase" along a steep canyon side hill. Wow, we won't even have to worry about slipping or even getting tired. And when we find him hunkering down up in a twisted old juniper tree,

we'll shake paws and hands and laugh. I'll bet that big cat will say, "You found me this time, but next time I'll sure give you the slip."

And let's get down on our hands and knees and watch the ants work. Maybe we'll find some answers to deep questions we've pondered, like: "How many ants does it take to drag a soup-bug up the side of an anthill?" And, "Do they work in shifts?"

I propose our joining up together to take care of the forests and streams over there. I've already spoken for that job, and I know you'll be there too. You can be in the "Streams and Fish Department," and I will work in the "Puma and Saber-tooth Tiger Department." Tell me, how do those big cats eat grass?

In the evenings we'll sit around our campfire and swap stories like we've done so many times in the past. Now tell me, dear friend, do we have to tell exact weights and measures over there, or can we speculate a little?

Do you still snore at night? I reckon I won't have to wake you up any more with, "Did you hear that?" and then try to beat you back to sleep while you're busy listening. I won't be bringing my earplugs.

Thank you, Glenn, for so many rich memories. You've got a head start on me again, just like you often did down here. But I'll be a catching up, and we'll hug and talk again soon. As you can plainly see, I didn't have to put a date on this letter. How handy.

I send you much love.

Your friend, Ken

LOVED BY PETS

Love often communicates in intense ways between us humans and our animal friends. I personally have known and learned much from this. I cherish these memories. Following are some of the many stories I have heard while working as a Klamath Hospice medical director that may give you added joy. (Names and places and some details are altered to protect privacy.)

Angel

Roy was dying of a slowly progressive neurological disorder, similar to Lou Gehrig's disease. As a physician working for Klamath Hospice I was asked to see Roy at his washing machine and appliance store. Was he in need of hospice care? His son, Dave, had come to run the business, and Roy liked to still come down to the store and sit in his brown easy chair. He was accompanied by his tiny fuzzy dog, Angel. I found them sitting close together in that soft chair. Dave brought over a small armchair for me. Roy's voice was almost inaudible, but Angel's welcome was to jump up behind me as I sat down to talk with Roy. She squirmed about and then leapt across to Roy's lap, pushing his oxygen line to one side. Roy weakly reached out and patted her head. She licked his hand and crowded close.

Roy's disease had rapidly progressed. There was concern that in spite of his now only being able to take a few steps using a walker, Angel, in her insistence on staying close, might cause him to fall. When Roy wore his soft slippers with woolly lining, the little dog would play with his shuffling feet, nipping at those fleecy critters. Thankfully a fall did not occur. As the disease rapidly progressed, it was soon impossible for Roy to go to the store with his son. He wanted Angel to be with him. They stayed home together. Roy died on a blustery spring day. Dave and the hospice nurse anticipated this and waited there with him. Oxygen no longer helped. His shallow breathing stopped. Angel, waiting nearby, jumped up on the bed and kissed his face.

Later, when the undertaker and his assistant arrived, they gently placed Roy on a stretcher and moved toward the door. Through the open doorway the stretcher was rolled across the short walk and lifted up the steep steps to a waiting hearse. Angel, Dave, and the nurse, along with watching pine trees, cedars, and junipers, all stood quietly. As the stretcher was being placed in the back of the hearse, the deeply reverent stillness was broken. Angel jumped from Dave's arms, rushed up the hillside steps and jumped in beside her master. Slowly Dave walked up those same steps, picked up the little dog, held her close, and wept.

Now, months later, Angel accompanies Dave to work. She will occasionally greet a visitor but mostly likes to rest in Roy's soft brown chair. It certainly has a special meaning for this little white dog.

Cats

Naomi was a lover of cats, and her new home in Pine Grove had become a haven for nearly thirty feral cats. She had been under hospice care for several days and had peacefully declined as expected. Each time when an aide or nurse arrived, the cats would scatter from the stranger. Some peeked from their retreats—most stayed well-hidden, restrained by fear from their distant past.

The family had phoned Becky, the hospice nurse, only moments before. It appeared that Naomi had stopped breathing. Parking her gray Suburu, she clutched her medicine bag and hurried up the orange brick walk separating rows of red and white petunias. It crossed a green lawn leading to a white bungalow surrounded by pines. She knew what she'd likely find.

Naomi's daughter opened the front door before Becky reached it. Several family members waited in the front room with teary eyes. Becky nodded and hurriedly followed the daughter to the nearby bedroom. The patient had indeed stopped breathing, but this room was crowded with cats. Now they did not run and indeed one long-haired yellow cat crowded close to his rescuer's face. Becky reached out a hand and stroked his long fur. He glanced up briefly then looked back at Naomi.

A family member said, "This is all most unusual." All that day the cats had stayed close to the dying lady. They no longer ran when a stranger appeared. "It was as if they were holding a wake."

Bandit

Bandit did his own thing. A little black dog with a slightly gray muzzle, he liked to be petted by Gregg, who was now dying of a stroke. But generally Bandit just stayed out of people's way. He was the house dog in their log home near Keno.

Two days previously the hospice social worker had seen Gregg's wife put Bandit out in the yard, the domain of their large brown hunting dog. The big dog just lifted a leg and peed on Bandit.

But Bandit had been very different on this day. He climbed up on the hospital-type bed and lay on his master's lap all that morning. He stayed there until evening, only jumping down once to get a drink of water. Shortly after Jill, the hospice nurse, arrived, Gregg passed on. It was a very peaceful death. As Gregg, surrounded by walls adorned with waterfowl and horns from past adventures, took his final weak breath, Bandit, yet on Gregg's lap, sat up, looked around, and then seemed to peer steadily off into the distance. Gregg's wife and daughter said Bandit had never acted like that before. Together they wondered, hugged Jill, and thanked her profusely.

Ted

Ted was a big black dog who was very devoted to Will. He had stayed close by through the last three years of his master's illness. Ted would go in and out through a hole the family had made in the screen door. Will would reach down and scratch his ears.

That July day as many gathered grieving over their father and friend's passing, the nurse noted that the old black dog stood nearby and trembled. He seemed to understand. She reached down and scratched his ears for several minutes.

Other Pets

Hal's daughter came to live with and care for him in his last days. He lived in one of several small one-bedroom homes in the area called "Mills Addition." His old dog slept on the bed beside him. The daughter, needing to be close and knowing the love between Hal and his old dog, elected to sleep nearby on the floor.

Sally's nurse said the patient had obviously loved animals. Hospice had arranged a hospital bed in the patient's living room. Three cages of finches spoke to her from nearby. A gray cat slept just above her head, and a little Chihuahua slept close by her feet. Her "family" loved her as she loved them. The "family" was large.

Earl was quite a gentleman. He'd been a platoon leader in the Vietnam War and said, "None of my platoon died." He loved to walk remote trails in the hills around Klamath Falls and would traverse many miles at a time. He often saw the tracks of cougar or bear. Sadie, his dog, walked with him.

As cancer spread and no further treatments became possible, he was placed in hospice care. Treatment of Earl also included care of Sadie. He lived in a small third-story apartment, and it eventually became impossible for him to take her for even short walks.

Before he died, he asked his hospice social worker if she would look after his dear dog. Allison, the social worker, was able to do this. Sadie remains in a very loving home. Wouldn't it be interesting to look inside Sadie's mind and see those warm memories?

Birch

Birch is a middle-aged border collie that was very attached to John. As John's cancer progressed, Birch seemed to want to stay closer. When I visited the first time, John's wife put the reluctant dog into a downstairs room. I could hear the continuous though distant bark. He'd rather be with John.

A few weeks later as our patient was near death, Kathy, our nurse, drove up the little street near Chiloquin, parked by the juniper shrubs, ascended the short cement walk, and tapped on the maroon front door. John's wife, Norma, escorted her to the upstairs bedroom.

Birch was lying on the pink and yellow flowered quilt beside John and arose as the nurse approached. Kathy changed direction to approach from the opposite side, but the border collie also went to the other side, keeping between the nurse and his dying master. Kathy, of course, stopped. The collie reached down and licked John's face.

Captain

All who helped care for Sibyl also noted Captain, her large sixteen-year-old rottweiler, lying on a rug near the foot of her bed. Captain, thin, ribs prominent and head gray, seldom moved. However, Catherine, our hospice nurse, reported that, the day Sibyl died, the very elderly dog had placed himself across the doorway of the small bedroom. He very much impeded entry. When the undertaker arrived, they gently moved the old dog. Pleading eyes turned upward.

The family told Catherine that they mercifully intended to have Captain put to sleep. He would also be cremated, and his ashes would be mixed and scattered with those of his soul mate in an area where they both loved to walk.

Blackie

Blackie became my dog in his puppyhood when I carried him chewing on my hand down the tarry road to our home. He smelled of brown gravy. We had many adventures through the years until the time I was in college and mostly away from home. Blackie became ill with paralysis of his hindquarters and passed away to his "better place."

A few days later I went with my parents to visit a dear aunt and uncle near Bend, Oregon. In my sadness with Blackie gone, I decided I'd go rabbit hunting among the lava hills with their junipers and sagebrush just west of Bend. As I traipsed into those hills an Irish setter came out of the brush and obviously wanted to go with me. I shooed him with several "Go homes" and chunked a few rocks in his direction. He'd go off a ways, sit down, and wait 'til I'd move on, and then rejoin me. I finally gave up the "shooing," and we had a most excellent time hunting rabbits there among the mahogany, junipers, and sagebrush. His being with me really perked me up. As we later returned near the edge of town, he vanished, just as he had come.

UGANDA

Many years ago the area now named Uganda was divided into fourteen closely related kingdoms. Its favorable climate, ideal altitude, and plentiful rainfall made it attractive to African cultivators and herders for hundreds of years. Centuries of cultivation removed most of the original tree cover there and around Lake Victoria. As the populace multiplied, a form of government developed, led by clan chiefs. During the nineteenth century several European powers contended over this area of Africa. Years of bloody conflict ensued—some were settled by machine guns, some were settled through monetary compensation, and others through negotiation. In 1894 the Uganda Protectorate was established under Britain, and lasted until 1962. Both large challenges and progress shaped the new country. Uganda was given complete independence from Britain in October 1962. Milton Obote, a political activist, became prime minister. Obote's government was ousted in a military coup in January 1971 by the armed forces commander, Idi Amin Dada. Amin gave himself titles: his excellency president for life, field marshal al hadji, Dr. Idi Amin, VC, DSO, MC, king of Scotland, lord of all the beasts of the earth and fishes of the sea, and conqueror of the British Empire in Africa. He initiated a reign of terror in which more than three hundred thousand Ugandans were murdered. Amin also invaded Tanzania, which in turn invaded Uganda with the help of Ugandan exiles. Amin fled to Libya in 1979.

Several interval leaders came and went until the present president, Yoweri Kaguta Musevini, came to power in 1986. Out of much turmoil in the late 1980s the Lord's Resistance Army was formed in northern Uganda by Joseph Kony. Child soldiers were forcibly recruited, villages were destroyed, thousands were killed, and terrible suffering ensued. About 1.2 million survived in refugee camps. It was into this devastation that MTI was asked to come to help strengthen many medical clinics.

SOLOMON—HIDDEN IN UGANDA

Solomon wore a wrinkled light-blue shirt and darker blue trousers with damaged sandals on his feet. As we loaded into our van, he climbed in beside me—thin, of medium height, and with weathered face—not the least imposing in appearance. We were leaving shortly to visit the first of several IDP (internally displaced people) camps in northern Uganda. Little did I expect to meet one of the major players in the history of this suffering part of Africa so soon.

Led by Joseph Kony, the LRA (Lord's Resistance Army) had been formed in this part of Uganda more than twenty years previously. Their alleged aim was to counter major wrongs being committed by the Ugandan government. But Kony and his followers forcibly recruited child soldiers, and soon years of devastation followed. Killings, beatings, rape, destroyed villages, and terrible fear ensued. Well over a million refugees became part of the picture. Kidnappings resulted to as many as twenty thousand children forced to be Kony's soldiers. The Anglican Diocese of Northern Uganda, centered at Gulu, suffered intensely, including the murder of the bishop's son.

As Kony's forces retreated, pressed by the Ugandan military and aided by other countries, the Northern Diocese started organizing ways of helping the thousands of suffering refugees. They selected Solomon to establish clinics, and he started them in ten different IDP camps. He also requested an international group called MAP (Medical Assistance Programs) to help. They in turn asked MTI (Medical Teams International) to visit the clinics and offer ideas for improving care. Our MTI crew consisted of Otto, an emergency room nurse and paramedic; Lou, a physician's assistant (PA-C); and myself, an internist. We each had years of medical experience both at home and in many parts of the world. I had been with Otto teaching Iraqis emergency medicine five years before, and Lou had been honored as our country's outstanding PA-C in the recent past. Susan, from the United States, and Mike, from Kenya, were those representing MAP, who very capably cared for us.

What a privilege to sit beside Solomon and hear his story. He was born at Anaka, a tiny town west of Gulu, part of the Acholi tribe. His parents had nine children, including seven girls. Four sisters preceded him, resulting in the name Solomon Okeny. ("Okeny" meaning "the only boy among the girls.") His father was a policeman. As a tiny boy he recalled often running and running in fear of some animals and of blood. Among the many wild animals near his village were water buffalo. He remembered being told to fall down and lay very still if they got too close. Once this happened—he did this and, "They jumped right over me." He recalls a house with thatched roof burning, killing six goats and a child. He pointed out a gnarled old tree from which, as a boy, he'd seen the hanging body of a man. He remembered the happiness when his father brought him brown shoes and a watch. "I was the only one in the whole village with brown shoes. I was proud. Everyone wanted to try them on. I attended the Anglican Church in Anaka and experienced baptism in my brown leather shoes. First they shaved my head, and then poured water on my head three times—'In the name of the Father, and the Son, and the Holy Spirit.' This was the customary way to do it.

"I went to school in Anaka—both primary and secondary. Then I did three years of religious education here at the Northern Ugandan Diocese. Later a Canadian NGO, working with the diocese, took me to Nairobi, Kenya, for several months of medical education. I became a priest, wanted to be a doctor, but didn't make it. Later I was invited to the Gulu Diocese for three years. Had four children at that time and have nine now. Five are yet at home in school. My mother is ninety years old—a very rare age in Uganda. I came to

Gulu in 1991. Our church had only one health center then. Now there are ten. I helped start them all."

We traveled in the edge of the bush, following a very primitive winding road and approaching an IDP camp near Anaka called Wii Anaka. Solomon continued—"LRA rebels came to this region in 1987. I often went out to this area. At first I lived with the rebels. I would tell them, 'This is not good.' During that time I had secretly taken ten rebel child soldiers on my motorcycle back to Gulu. One I hid in my house under the bed for nearly two months. Then the rebels started talking against me. They burned up my motorcycle. My wife asked me, 'Why are you doing this?'

"Even in the edge of Gulu we would often hear gunshots at night. The area near the bishop's house became mostly controlled by rebels, and the Ugandan military would also sometimes fire on us. The rebels usually killed with clubs and machetes, but one night they did shoot the bishop's son. The rebels started withdrawing from the area in 2005 and by last summer, 2006, were mostly gone.

"Now the rebels are centered in a remote area of Congo, with some scattered into other nearby countries. Killing and eating wildlife comprises a significant part of their food. Bishop Nelson Onono-Onweng has made a difficult trip to talk with Joseph Kony, trying to persuade him to take a better path."

A few days later we traveled many kilometers eastward from Gulu to a very remote clinic in a large IDP camp at Dino. Roads were winding, very narrow, and covered in mud and pools of dirty water. The country reached higher, swathed by both dense bushes and trees. In one large area, pine trees had been planted—now about fifty feet in height. Close to Dino we saw a few garden areas near the road.

Solomon told me, "This is where Kony grew up, started gathering soldiers and began fighting in 1986. His Acholi people want him to give up his terrible ways and come home. They want to forgive him." He then continued to tell me, "When villages are fighting other villages or tribes, it has been our custom for the chiefs to bring their best spears, put them together, bend the handles and forgive each other. They do this even if there has been much killing. Then peace can return. This is what we want to do with Joseph Kony."

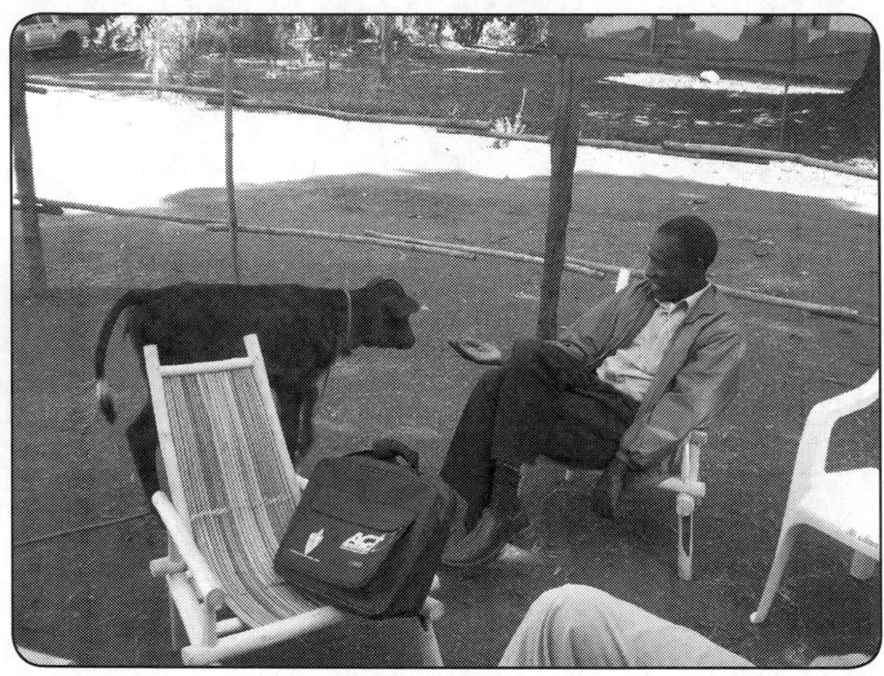

I later learned that for each individual's forgiveness and atonement there are two phases: first, the aggressor must give a full description of the crimes committed; second, the aggressor must negotiate regarding compensation in as much as possible. These are monitored by tribal elders.

LEARNING UGANDAN WAYS

Downpours of rain had flooded us for several days. These seasonal rains added to travel problems for our medical team, Lou, Otto and myself, but also brought unforeseen insights. We had been surprised by the immensity of anthills, some reaching as high as eight feet, and some of their occupants' astonishing ways. When traveling to and from a distant site, they form two dense rows of ants traveling side by side but moving in opposite directions. After very hard rains came to the area, flying ants swarmed the skies. We saw children and adults with small containers moving quickly and snatching about in the grass and bushes along the roads. We, of course, asked, and found they were catching the flying ants and putting them in cans—a delicacy to eat at home with their families.

Lou didn't let it rest with that information. Back at the "Sheraton" (The sign we placed over our front door at Otto's suggestion), he expanded his front porch tea drinking and caught a few of the flying ants. To handle the ants, he had to kill them or pull off their wings, and reported, "The smaller bugs have a crunchy feeling, and taste something like a chip. The larger ants are juicier but have a bitter taste that is far from pleasant. Both have hard wings that stick in your teeth and are a bugger to get out." *I could tell by the look on his face which variety he was eating. Later he learned that the Ugandans remove the wings and cook the bugs before eating them.*

The Anglican Diocese of Northern Uganda had several houses, a school, and a church just north of Gulu. We certainly appreciated getting to stay in one of their houses. Prior to arrival we were told that it had electricity and running water and a bathroom with regular sit-down toilets. What we found was different, but we had no complaints. Future indoor water was planned, but so far only available via the running legs of Ugandan ladies who carried buckets or five-gallon cans on their heads. The toilet tanks used some of that "running water." We did get electricity, but totally unpredictably. Our tiny kitchen area became very usable by bringing a propane hot plate from Kampala. We loved being there: talking, joking, planning together, and frequently visiting with passersby. In addition to people this included goats, fat-tailed sheep, cattle, chickens, and guinea hens. Our "lawn" never needed mowing. It was "fenced" with piles of small limbs that didn't slow down a dashing bull with a loose rope around its neck, being pursued by three young boys. We were glad it didn't decide to turn in at our front door.

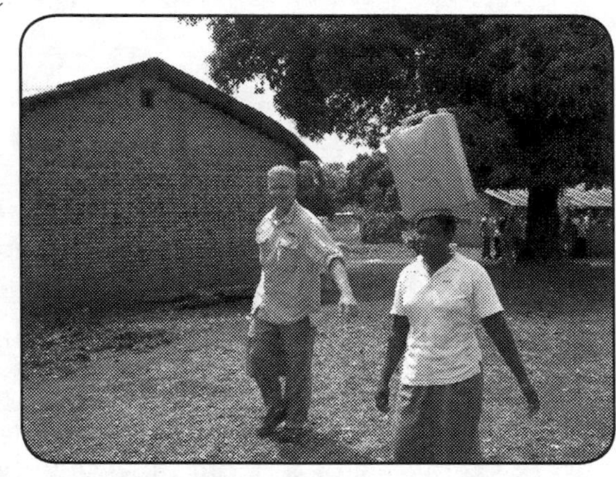

Agnes, a young lady who came during the day, did a superb job of cleaning house and cooking for us. She had been under the bishop and his wife's care for about three years. Her family lived ten kilometers west of Gulu. They had been chased into hiding in the bush several times while trying to evade Kony's militants. Her brother experienced a violent capture, and they had not heard of him since. One of the ploys of the LRA (Lord's Resistance Army) is to change the names of those they forcibly recruit. Those captured usually are given options—such as joining the LRA or having ears and lips cut off or being hacked and beaten to death. Is he alive? Five years have passed, and no one knows. Agnes was shy. At first she seemed reluctant to eat with us after fixing our evening dinner, but finally consented to do so on a few occasions. She is finishing high school, and we heard just before leaving that she had been accepted into a small college in Gulu. She plans to teach. She will do well.

As in many tropical areas, the "Sheraton" was rich in wildlife, including large scrambling cockroaches, many spiders and lizards, and armies of termites. They liked our backpacks and clothes. As we prepared to leave Uganda, Otto found they'd devoured his Pepto-Bismol. Our tiny front porch was often visited by enormous bees resembling bumblebees, but much larger. One morning we noted an abrupt decline in their numbers and found colorful fuzzy bodies scattered around. It was a puzzle without answers.

Next to our house was the home of Bishop Onono-Onweng and his wife. He was deeply concerned for the thousands of displaced and hurting people in this part of Uganda. We had the pleasure of visiting with him and his wife several times. She served us tea and some "nibbles." On their living room wall hung a framed UNESCO Peace Prize, given to the bishop in recognition of his efforts to bring peace to Uganda. Here are some of the concerns he expressed to us:

"Trauma has terribly influenced both young and old and all those in between.

"Aggression occurs without any reason."

"Suicide is common."

"Fighting among the youth thrives. Killing is not a problem for them."

"Where are the men?"

"Many men have run away from the IDP camps—often alcohol is involved."

"Cultural and moral values—lost! No respect for themselves or others."

"There are a lot of child mothers. Many of them also died during childbirth."

"Countless children have been produced during the war. They roam the camps without supervision. Thousands of children in northern Uganda do not go to school."

"Most people have no value for God in their lives. Many say, 'Your God is sleeping. Where is He?'"

"Poverty is extreme. So many innocents have suffered and have been killed."

"However, the people have a high spirit to survive. Some are trying to start small businesses. We keep a girl who had no money and have kept several others. Some of the other ways we are trying to help include:

"Doing counseling and helping several NGOs (nongovernment organizations) work with the refugees in areas of posttraumatic stress. We are setting up three separate villages where this will take place.

"We are also starting a small vocational school.

"Thank you for helping with our health clinics. HIV and AIDS are rampant.

"We are starting to train refugees in modern practices of farming.

"We want more technical assistance to help them work with their hands."

"I talked with a UN lady who pronounced, 'Justice must prevail.' The UN is insistent that Kony stand trial. We feel our Acholi African system is better. How can we merge it with the feelings of the UN? Now Uganda is also trying to implement the traditional system of justice. The World Court opposes it.

"The native system is that of forgiveness. This war is not the typical war, and we do wonder if the traditional system will work. Kony can come home to live with us. From the Christian perspective we have to believe in the God of forgiveness.

"One primary architect of the LRA surrendered and is now in Gulu. He had to go through a time of showing his heart change, and then became a free man.

"I went to visit Kony several months ago in the Congo. Many of his child soldiers are yet in southern Sudan. Sudan has supplied funds and food to ask the LRA to oppose the Southern Sudanese forces. Kony received me graciously and said, 'It is now time to talk peace around the world. It is like a cockfight—so it must now end.'

As an alternative to staying in southern Sudan, I encouraged all the LRA forces to go to remote areas in the Congo. But they started demanding money before moving to the Congo bush."

(Info recorded and written in 2007—Ken Magee)

> *March 18, 2011:*
>
> *Kony subsequently refused to return to face the UN World Court. The LRA yet roams a remote area near the size of California that straddles three countries, (Democratic Republic of Congo, Congo, and Sudan), making it difficult for a single national army to hunt them down. Since December of 2007, OCHA, the UN's Office for Coordination of Humanitarian Affairs, estimates the group has killed more than two thousand people and abducted twenty-six hundred in Congo, where they sought refuge from the Ugandan Army in 2005. They have intensified attacks in northeastern Democratic Republic of Congo this year and have left dozens dead.*
>
> *Excerpts from article by Michael J. Cavanaugh <www.bloomberg.com/news>*

Early in our stay at the "Sheraton," Solomon, the primary force in creating health clinics, told this story about the bishop:

> Two and a half years before, a refugee from the bush area of northeastern Uganda journeyed to tell Bishop Onono-Onweng of their desperate plight. The messenger's words: "Thousands of my Acholi people have been driven from our homes in the bush, and now we are starving and dying with disease. Our food has been taken, our livestock have been killed and our homes burned. We are suffering rape and murder." The bishop decided he must go and see for himself.

Solomon continued:

> The bush had been engulfed in much fighting between the LRA and the Ugandan military. It had been coinhabited by both the LRA and many small villages, now destroyed. Most surviving people existed in an IDP (internally displaced people) camp called Omee II. The military had recently bulldozed a small but lengthy and winding road into the area for use to help fight the rebels.
>
> After driving his car westward many kilometers, the bishop came to the beginning of the small military road. Soldiers were guarding its entrance and strongly refused to allow him to go on. The bishop said, "You can shoot me if you wish, but I'm going on," and proceeded to drive around the roadblock. They did not shoot but sent two soldiers with him.
>
> The messenger had been correct. The bishop found deplorable conditions—people in utmost poverty, starving and dying of many diseases. He, along with me and others, brought in clothes and food, and wells were dug for safe water; their pump handles worked almost constantly. We enlisted help from MAP (Medical Assistance Programs) and started a clinic at Omee II a year ago. Several heroic men and women came to work in the yet danger-encircled health clinic. The site sat in the edge of a Ugandan Forest Reserve. Later the camp will need relocation.

How well I remember our first of several trips to Omee II. As our day started at the "Sheraton" we sat on its tiny front porch waiting for our car and driver. The temperature was down in the midseventies and the sky was light blue. We felt a gentle breeze and popcorn-like clouds drifted eastward—a beautiful day. We waited to take the long trek to Omee II.

It took us about two and a half hours to navigate nearly seventy miles of long and bumpy road in our four-wheel-drive vehicle. Jungle and thick bushes crowded close. Cicadas sang lustily in the areas of thick brush. Two monkeys scurried across the road and disappeared.

On arrival at the IDP camp, Omee II, children with big tummies and very thin arms and legs ran to meet us. In general their mood, as well as that of the adults, seemed even more somber than we'd encountered in most IDP camps. Some were sweeping the bare ground between their closely packed grass-roofed mud huts with small homemade brooms. Much good had happened, but it obviously remained a very needy area. These people had nowhere else to go. Their homes in the bush had been destroyed.

On our return from that first long trip to Omee II, our vehicle's engine started missing and then lost power as we arrived back at our home base, the "Sheraton." It quit and could not be restarted. We were so thankful this had not happened far out in the bush.

In visiting the several IDP camps repeatedly, we were able to work and talk with the very capable, hardworking nursing assistants in each camp. Many needs were unmistakable to us, but we asked repeatedly what *they* saw as their needs and what they envisioned for the future. These health workers' dreams for the future often included simple things such as "a bicycle" (from one who had to travel many miles to get from his home to the clinic). But by far the biggest request was "more training." At that point their diagnosis and treatment centered primarily around a few ailments such as malaria and cellulitis. We had brought along and gave them several books on tropical medicine and started the process of bringing in medical people with backgrounds that could be used in furtherance of their medical training. We also introduced and started working toward some simple laboratory testing, such as dipstick urine testing, and simple blood tests, including testing for HIV and checking for anemia and diabetes.

Most of the tiny buildings needed more space and waiting areas with roofs to shield from sun and rain. On first walking into the clinic called "Wii Anaka," we found a single room crowded with both waiting people and those being examined. There existed no privacy to talk and minimal space for examining patients. Medicines were brought from a central pharmacy in Gulu—plenteous in amount and variety but not well sorted or distributed adequately. We talked with workers from MAP, who proceeded to correct this medication bottleneck and supervised the building of a covered waiting area outside of the examining room.

Together with the nursing assistants we saw many memorable patients.

A ten-year-old girl had the entirety of both legs charred from boiling water—third- and fourth-degree burns. We were so pleased to have Lou along with his experience in burn centers. He not only carefully treated those horrendous, potentially lethal burns, pulling away dead tissue, washing and applying antibacterial solutions, and covering with sterile dressings, but also taught a young male nursing assistant how to care for the girl in the days to follow. A week later we again came back to the camp, and she was doing excellently with the nursing assistant's help. That handsome young man rightfully seemed pleased with his care. More than a life was saved.

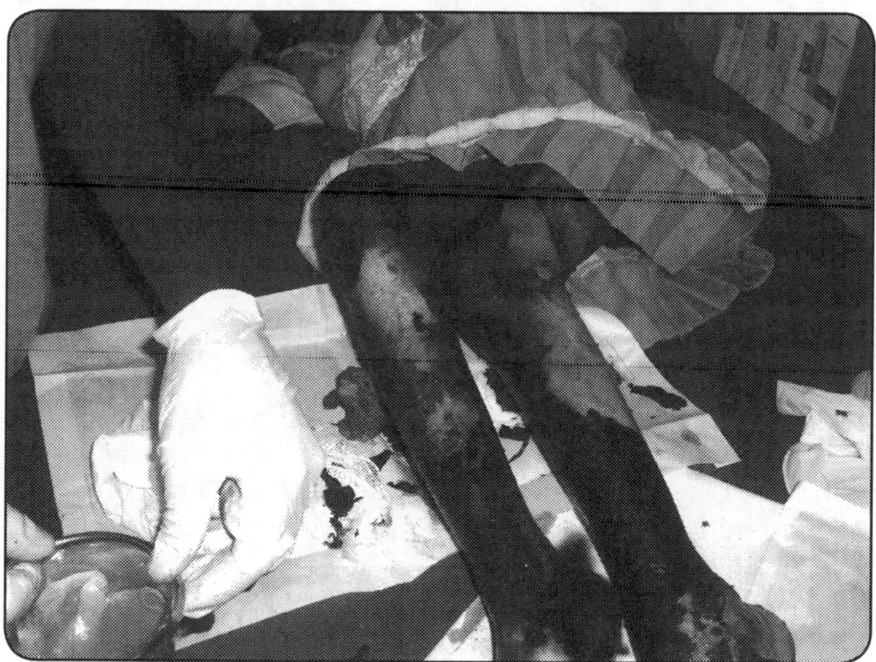

A frantic mother ran into one clinic dangling her little boy by the ankles. He was very ill with severe diarrhea and vomiting. The little guy had also choked on some vomitus. This was right down Otto's line of expertise, and he took over. Again he was able to show a nursing assistant some of the things to do.

Many other particular patients cross my mind. Some needed help in a facility not available for those out in the Ugandan bush: a ten-year-old girl deformed by huge ever-expanding facial veins; a lady who came crawling to our clinic because of an animal bite resulting in a leg fracture and deep bone infection; an infant, brought by her grandmother, born less than a day before, complicated by aspiration at birth and a very congested lung. In each of these situations we started both treatment and planning, with hope for their futures.

We will never forget what we both heard and experienced and hopefully passed on to the Ugandan nursing assistants. The list is long.

VIOLENCE—I DON'T HAVE AN ANSWER

Duane's Memories, 2010, an Interview by Ken Magee

K: And that's a good summary type statement—"I don't have an answer." Lots of people would relate to that thought, but let me go back with you a ways. Where did you grow up?

D: I grew up near Yakima, Washington.

K: And if you could describe your childhood and teen years, what were they like?

D: Well, like all kids we ran around, played baseball in the summer, worked in the orchards, bucked hay. We were on the outskirts of the city, so we were essentially like farm kids. Several of us kids would get together, you know, four or five on a side, right field closed, both slow-pitch and fast-pitch ball. Then we'd get together and play kids from other neighborhoods.

In the sixties I was in junior high and high school. The grades were ninth, tenth, eleventh, and twelfth. Public schools had junior high, but Catholic schools had first through eighth and then high school. I went to Catholic school through the tenth grade, then to public school. My dad was a mechanic, and I got to hang around him in a gas station garage.

K: Do you remember when you began to hear about the Vietnam War?

D: Let's see. Was that about when Kennedy was shot? It would have been about '62 or '63.

K: What were your thoughts?

D: Just that I was more aware of it—that we were involved in Asia.

K: Were you drafted or did you volunteer to go to Vietnam? How did that come about?

D: I didn't have any money to go to college. I wasn't married in '64. Everybody knew that without something to defer them they were going to get drafted. There was no lottery. Everybody who was graduating from high school got drafted if they didn't have a handicap or some type of exemption. They might join the National Guard or air force or something.

K: Do you remember your thoughts about getting drafted?

D: My thoughts—I thought it was the funniest thing in the world. I got this letter that I kept for years: 'Greetings from President Johnson. Your friends and neighbors have volunteered you …'

K: When you left, were you happy to leave? Were you scared?

D: Like a lot of guys, there were a lot of us, and we wanted to go over there.

K: Do you have other memories of what you were thinking of, or expecting?

D: When we grew up it was always like the Saturday movies. We'd go to the matinees. It was like John Wayne whupping the Japs, like John Wayne whupping the Germans, Audie Murphy getting on a tank in France and stopping the enemies. All those glorified World War II characters.

K: Do you remember landing in Vietnam and going to wherever your base was?

D: Yes. This was surreal stuff. I remember flying over Anchorage, flew to Tokyo and to Saigon. We had to stand on the tarmac for hours. We could barely make out this red-headed, white-dressed Ann Margaret doing a show about a mile away. And finally they put us on a bus with screens over the windows. We said, 'There are screens over the windows on this bus.' And we were told, 'That's so they can't throw a grenade into the bus.'

K: Where did you go from there?

D: I'm not sure that I want to go back to the awful things that happened then. Time in those villages was tough. Mostly I can't even talk about the horrors. Let's just skip those months.

I did see the bad treatment of those we were trying to help: people from villages that were destroyed—taken to refugee camps and then badly treated. I remember them having only dirty water to drink and some of us giving from our clean filtered water. We were commanded to not do that. Their water had hookworms and such and was filled with sewage. Many of them were getting sick and dying. They were supposedly our allies.

I came to realize that they wanted to be left alone to till the earth, to raise food, and to enjoy their families. They were just like us. The Vietnamese, especially the Viet Cong, they wanted freedom from first the Chinese and then the French and now the Americans and Western powers.

Certainly that really bothered me—the callousness of war. Some were in big wire cages and were given cans of food. They didn't know how to open the cans, and we tried to help. When we went in there to help, we were asked, 'What are you doing in there?'

We're trying to show them how to open the cans. They wouldn't let us. It was sort of like the dirty water.

And when I came back home we were met by some who called us, 'Baby killers.' Others would ask, 'How did it feel to pull the trigger? Wasn't it a great feeling?' And I was very upset. I just wanted to forget."

K: We talked a bit about the question, "Are there solutions to this type of thing?"

D: "I don't know. These things are so very difficult to talk about."

(Following this it indeed was very difficult for Duane to talk. There were short bits of thought, but background noise in the little restaurant made it difficult to hear my recording. We decided it was best to stop at that point—perhaps to go on at a later time.)

Several weeks later our paths crossed, and I had the privilege of continuing to hear Duane's memories. Pauses were long. It was very difficult for him.

Here are his comments:

> I came to Vietnam by myself and I left by myself—tried to form some bonds, but they were soon broken. You're afraid all the time. Everyone told you, "If you don't get too close, you won't get hurt." That's why we mostly used nicknames or first names.
>
> Our treatment of our Vietnamese allies was despicable. In the first place you often couldn't tell who was friend or foe. Most of them just wanted to be left alone with their family—to farm their two acres. I tried to give food and water to them when I could, but we weren't supposed to. We could get water from a nearby river for them, but not clean water. It was so dirty that for us swimming was forbidden—but we

could give it to them to drink. I'll never get that out of my mind. It haunts me yet.

A Viet Cong man was blown to bits right by our camp. On patrol we passed him every day. We were shown how to treat the body parts—to rub cigarettes out on his face, to smear peanut butter on other parts; ants would be attracted. We were forbidden to bury him. I couldn't stand it. I finally sneaked out at night and buried him. If I'd told what I'd done, my sergeant or lieutenant would have really got on me.

I had it different than most GIs. I played with the kids and visited the old people. Most didn't do that and called me a 'gook lover.' But the villagers and farmers were people just like us in America. Most soldiers stayed away from the villages. I learned some Vietnamese words in their language for "sit down," "careful," "please," "go there," "thank you," and "wait here." I sat in their houses, played cards and ate meals with them. Most GIs didn't. I think my growing up working along with migrants in Washington State helped.

Sometimes we had to move Vietnamese to safer places by helicopter. We tried to get them on the aircraft, but they wouldn't go. I learned to pick up a pig and then board, and after that they would follow.

It was terrible having my fellow soldiers blown to bits. With the first one, I tried to put him back together. I was so relieved when the medics came. This was very tough—I wonder what happened to him?

Not every soldier in 'Nam was a killer. A few guys get a big adrenalin rush in killing other people. Some don't want to do it, but do it anyway. Many just hunker down and shoot into the sky.

When I returned home it seemed that only my family had any respect for me. I yet have flashbacks. More than twenty years later I was standing at the top of the stairs leading down to the laundry room. We all loved plants, and that room was surrounded with overflowing shelves and hanging pots of indoor plants. It was twilight and window light was dim. My daughter, Allison, and her Asian friend, Alisha, were just leaving the laundry room, turned off its light and started up the stairs. Looking through all that greenery, I suddenly saw the Viet Cong and launched myself down the stairs toward them. My daughter's scream, "Dad! What are you doing?" brought me back to reality. Terror had returned. I was back in Vietnam. It was very real.

Even yet flashbacks, like sounds or smells, suddenly propel me back there. Nobody much understands. They just think "*You are a jerk*" when you yell or do something strange. There's got to be another way.

My point of view is that there has got to be a better way than violence. I think "fight or flight" are neither good. I'm not going to change the whole world, but if I'm with you and you're bad-mouthing the Indians, the Germans, or Africans or someone else, I'm going to disagree. If you don't stop, then I'll get up and walk away. I don't want to just sit there with my mouth closed.

THE FINAL QUESTION

"The family is extremely important." This was his answer.

I had asked Frank, who is very aware of the limited days ahead for him, "If today you could tell young people the very most important thing, what would it be?"

Frank has suffered from Waldenstrom's macroglobulenemia (a form of cancer) and chronic lung disease for many years. In the last two years he has declined in an ability to work in his garden area and make many superb Native American works of art. He is now becoming totally chair- and couch-bound. A few steps bring on marked weakness and shortness of breath.

Mason City, Iowa, welcomed Frank in 1939. His father was from Tennessee and of Cherokee Indian descent and was a traveling musician. During his first four years, Frank and his Irish Catholic mother traveled with his dad. Sadly, the father was an alcoholic and often beat his mother. They divorced.

Frank stated, "I was mostly raised by women in Iowa, especially my aunt Margaret, who was a first-grade teacher. We lived in farming country, where families often got together and helped each other.

"My early learning included a mixture of Catholic and Native American thoughts. I especially liked the Native American spiritualism—the idea of being one with my Creator.

"I wish we could learn sooner. In my fifties I went on a vision quest. I followed the way of the Lakota Sioux, traveling to a remote hill, where I stayed without food or water four days and nights. Food and water had been left with me, but it was for the Spirits. The quest was called 'going on the hill.' I was crying for a vision. I asked God to get our estranged families back together. On about the second or third day I felt confusion and wondered, 'Why would anyone do this?' I had to refocus.

"After four days the elders came to get me. They poured the water on the ground. They said, 'Share whatever you choose to share. It may take a long time to get clarity on what you have learned.' They then escorted me to the sweat lodge. I was allowed to drink water there and afterward was given a small meal.

"In the next year, indeed the family started getting closer. Most of my family had died, so it was mostly my wife Paula's side of the family. One relative arrived to visit for the first time in thirty years. The closeness has continued."

Frank related, "Here are some of the things of which I have become convinced: The earth is not ours—we are of the earth. It is what we have done for others that will be remembered. Do unto others as you would have them do to you—doing for rather than doing to. We need to communicate what love really is. We must give our children a loving childhood."

Frank went through some tumultuous years with alcohol, but did get back on track, went further in school, and worked for many years in Chicago area hospitals as a respiratory therapist.

Paula Grey Wolf Clapper has journeyed with Frank now for many years. They have much respect and sharing. They, together, are superb Native American artists. Paula's family became Frank's family. It was most meaningful to him when his stepdaughter asked, "Can I call you dad?"

With Frank's severe and progressive illness they have had major decisions. Their children live in Arizona, and in his thoughtful praying Frank has decided that his final and most meaningful act is to take Paula to live with her children. He needs continuous supplemental oxygen, and airlines would not take him. Facing two days of auto travel is daunting, but friends and family are helping. Frank says, "God gives me peace with this decision. Even if I don't arrive in Arizona, I will know that Paula has arrived where she now belongs."

BEYOND SURPRISE

Gearhart Mountain, just north of Bly, Oregon, marks the center of a wilderness area rich in challenges and unspoiled treasures. When Monna and her friend Mary Ann found a bit of time away from their demanding roles as registered nurses in Klamath Falls, they decided to unwind by experiencing these riches for three June days of camping. Their two eager dogs accompanied them. Monna and Mary Ann found more than anyone could have foreseen.

Gearhart is an ancient volcanic mountain with a large notch in its long summit. Primitive Indian stories describe a great boat landing there and seashells to be found. Monna had journeyed into this solitude several times and enjoyed its inner healing. But history also tells of children near its base on a Sunday school picnic blown apart by a Japanese balloon-delivered bomb, the only such deaths in the forty-eight American states during World War II. Even more recent history relates a thwarted attempt of Al Quaida to establish a nearby terrorist training camp.

Leaving their car at Lookout Trailhead, Monna tells of being awed by the blue sky above stately ponderosa and smaller jack pine. The smell of white fir and the beauty of new leaves adorning vine maple and aspen added richness. They found more snow than the Forest Service had predicted and eventually could not see the trail, but this was no problem. Crossing over to the north side of the mountain near the summit notch, they entered the drainage of Dairy Creek. Here, hanging meadows with bubbling springs and groves of light-barked aspen provided areas free of snow, and perfect places to camp. Bright yellow buttercups encircled these springs, and tiny frogs serenaded at night. Morel mushrooms tasted delicious in quick-cooking couscous. It was truly a healing place.

After two restful nights they started the trek out. Mary Ann's husband expected them home that evening; but up toward the summit they could not find the trail. The late spring snow was deep and soft. They searched and searched. Monna felt confused, and, as exhaustion settled in, she prayed quietly for God's help. Among trees at the bottom of a large, steep snowfield, they wondered about setting up camp for the night and attempting to get out the next day. Searchers would be alerted soon.

Monna relates that glancing up the slope they were startled to see a figure coming toward them. He was walking barefoot through deep snow. A serape covered most of his body, and he carried a packboard. In one hand was a homemade walking stick, nearly the same length as his medium height. He had a full beard and crewcut hair and appeared very neat and clean. The wood on the back of his homemade packboard was in the shape of a cross and about two feet in height. Monna wondered if it was intentional. She recalls that their two dogs acted oddly. The generally aggressive dog stood still and shook. The usually timid one approached the stranger with tail wagging. As he came near, Mary Ann exclaimed, "You aren't wearing shoes!"

He replied without accent, "I never wear shoes."

Monna asked, "Do you know where the trail is?"

He answered, "Right up this slope a fair ways."

As they parted the stranger said, "God bless you."

And Monna replied, "And you also."

Mary Ann and Monna followed the barefoot tracks up the steep snowy slope as the stranger journeyed on into the nearby forest. High above them they found blazes on trees marking the trail, and there the barefoot prints abruptly ended. The seven-mile return trip down to the trailhead and their car was made fairly quickly. No other car was there …

As I heard this unusual story from Monna, I wondered if Mary Ann would see things quite differently. I wanted to hear her separate perspective, and at a small restaurant she graciously related the following:

> While backpacking in the Gearhart Wilderness area, my friend and I became hopelessly lost, off trail, in deep snow. We spent nearly six hours scrambling up and down the face of the mountain trying to pick up the trail to the top of the summit—all to no avail. Exhausted, wet, and hungry, we stopped at a stream to rest, ration our food, and assess our situation. Daylight was waning along with our energy, so we charted a possible new course through the forest. If unsuccessful again, we would set up camp and wait for the rescue crew to escort us in the morning.
>
> Just as we embarked in a new direction, a man stepped out of the wilderness. He was barefoot, wearing white pants and a Mexican serape. He carried a small cloth knapsack with a two-foot wooden cross strapped to his back. He certainly looked incongruent with our surroundings. Though shocked by his appearance, we asked for directions and he stated he had just come off the trail, which crossed about five-hundred yards directly above where we stood.
>
> The forest was dense, the snow three to five feet deep, and we could not locate the trail in thousands of acres of wilderness. Yet here our paths intersected at an exact moment directly below our destination, one which had eluded us for the last six hours. Had he appeared twenty seconds later, we would have missed him and headed off in the wrong direction yet again. The miracle of his presence at that particular time defied explanation. Even more disquieting, his footprints in the snow disappeared after we reached the summit trail. No trace of his passing could

> be found on the remainder of the trail or at the trailhead.
>
> Questions overwhelmed us. Where had he come from? How had he navigated such rugged terrain and soft packed snow barefooted? How did he happen on us in the middle of nowhere at that precise moment? Answers eluded us. I was left with an experience that didn't fit neatly into my mental constructs.
>
> Perhaps this was my real-life opportunity to get comfortable with the uncomfortable—to step off into the abyss and face the challenge of remaining open to the possibility that something exists beyond what my logical mind can explain—and to trust that there is a Divine Force infusing this world and allow that truth to inform my life's journey.

Friends later checked with the Forest Service in Bly, but no one fitting the description of their helper had ever been seen.

DEEP THANKS

My deep thanks to Bas Vanderzalm and all his fellow workers at Medical Teams International. What wonderful help you have been in my journeys. I add this information out of much personal gratitude.

Medical Teams International is rated among the strongest and most efficient charities in the nation. Recently Charity Navigator rated Medical Teams International as one of its ten Top-Notch Charities among the five thousand evaluated. I am not surprised.

I love your stated purpose: "To demonstrate the love of Christ to people affected by disaster, conflict and poverty around the world."

I so admire your expressed values:

to serve needy people regardless of political affiliation
to avoid taking political stances
to welcome those of various faith backgrounds
to work together with partners, both expatriate and national
to be good stewards of the resources entrusted to us (Overall only a small percentage of funds are used in overhead. At least 95 percent goes into actual relief and development work.)

I appreciate the many volunteers who help both at home and around the world.

People interested in serving with Medical Teams International, either in the States or internationally can contact them at:

Volunteer opportunities: See website. www.medicalteams.org
e-mail: info@medicalteams.org

Headquarters in Portland, Oregon
Location:

Medical Teams International
14150 SW Milton Court
Tigard, OR 97224

Mailing Address: PO Box 10, Portland, OR 97207
Phone: Local—503-624-1000; toll free—800-959-4325
Office in Seattle, Washington, area:
Location:

Medical Teams International
9680 153rd Avenue Northeast
Redmond, WA 98052
Phone: 425-454-8326

Thank you again, MTI.
Ken Magee